# MALTA
## Travel Guide
## 2024

Discover the hidden gems of Malta and Gozo in this comprehensive travel guide, navigating through Valetta's cultural treasures, insider knowledge

Dominic Stone

All rights reserved. No part of this publication may be reproduced, distributed, or transmitted in any form or by any means, including photocopying, recording, or other electronic or mechanical methods, without the prior written permission of the publisher, except in the case of brief quotations embodied in critical reviews and certain other noncommercial uses permitted by copyright law.

Copyright © Dominic Stone,2023.

# TABLE OF CONTENTS

**INTRODUCTION**...........................................7
Geography and Location.....................8
History and Culture............................ 10
Malta's population............................. 16
Religious Practices in Malta............... 17

Chapter One....................................20
**Planning Your Trip**............................. 21
When to Visit Malta........................... 21
Visa and Entry Requirements........... 22
Currency and Budgeting................... 25
Language and Communication........ 28

Chapter Two....................................32
**Getting to Malta**...............................**33**
Flights to Malta.................................33
Transportation within Malta.............. 35
Airport Information.............................39
Public Transportation....................... 42

Chapter Three............................... 47
**Accommodation**...............................**48**
Types of Accommodation................48
Recommended Hotels and Resorts............... 50
Hostels and Guesthouses...............53
Vacation Rentals.............................. 56

Chapter Four..........................................59

**Exploring Malta's island top attractions..........59**

Top tourist cities to stay in Malta....................61

Historical Sites and Museums........................63

Beaches and Coastal Activities.......................65

Rural and Natural Attractions..........................66

Chapter Five............................................67

**Dining and Cuisine....................................67**

Maltese Food and Specialties........................67

Restaurants and Local Eateries......................68

Street Food and Markets...............................71

Dietary Preferences.....................................73

Chapter Six..............................................78

**Malta's Activities and Entertainment...............78**

Water Sports and Recreation..........................78

Hiking and Adventure...................................79

Nightlife and Entertainment............................81

Cultural Festivals........................................82

Chapter Seven..........................................85

**Shopping in Malta.....................................85**

Souvenirs and Local Crafts............................85

Popular Shopping Districts.............................86

Markets and Bazaars...................................88

Duty-Free Shopping....................................90

Chapter Eight............................................. 93
**Practical Information..................................... 93**
Health and Safety..................................93
Local Customs and Etiquette......................... 96
Emergency Contacts.................................101
Internet and Connectivity............................ 104

Chapter Nine............................................. 107
**Travel Tips and Resources........................... 107**
Packing Tips.......................................107
Money-Saving Strategies............................ 109
Travel Apps and Websites..........................112

Chapter Ten.............................................113
**Sample Itineraries.................................... 114**
3-Day Highlights of Malta........................... 114
Family-Friendly Trip...............................116
Off the Beaten Path Adventures...................119
Romantic Getaway.................................122

Chapter Eleven......................................... 126
**Beyond Malta...........................................126**
Day Trips to Gozo and Comino..................... 126
Exploring Nearby Destinations.....................128

Chapter Twelve........................................ 131
**Traveling Responsibly................................131**
Environmental Initiatives............................ 131
Responsible Tourism Tips........................... 133

Supporting Local Communities...................... 135
**CONCLUSION...............................................138**

# INTRODUCTION

Malta, an island nation located in the heart of the Mediterranean Sea, is a captivating blend of history, culture, and natural beauty. With a rich tapestry of influences from various civilizations, this small archipelago has a story that spans millennia. In this book, we will explore the enchanting world of Malta, from its ancient origins to its vibrant modern identity.

## Geography and Location

Malta, an European country, is situated in the central Mediterranean Sea, approximately 80 kilometers (50 miles) south of Sicily, Italy. It is part of the Maltese archipelago, which includes three main islands: Malta, Gozo, and Comino, as well as several smaller islets. Covering a total land area of just over 316 square kilometers, it is one of the world's smallest and most densely populated countries.

The Maltese landscape is characterized by rugged coastlines, limestone cliffs, and picturesque harbors. Its position in the Mediterranean has historically made it a strategic crossroads for trade, resulting in a unique blend of cultures and a diverse history.

Malta, an archipelago nestled in the heart of the Mediterranean Sea, is a captivating destination defined by its unique geography and strategic location. Comprising three main islands - Malta, Gozo, and Comino - as well as several smaller islets, Malta is an ideal blend of natural beauty and historical significance.

The archipelago is situated approximately 80 kilometers (50 miles) south of Sicily, Italy, and its strategic location has played a pivotal role throughout history. The islands' rocky coastlines, limestone cliffs, and picturesque harbors make for a stunning Mediterranean landscape. Malta covers a total land area of just over 316 square kilometers, making it one of the world's smallest and most densely populated countries.

Malta's geographical position has made it a crossroads for trade and cultural exchange for centuries. The unique blend of Mediterranean and European influences is evident in its culture, architecture, and cuisine.

## Natural Beauty and Climate

Malta's geography offers a diverse and breathtaking natural landscape. The islands boast crystal-clear waters, pristine beaches, and numerous sea caves. Comino's Blue Lagoon is famous for its vibrant turquoise waters, while Gozo is home to the stunning Azure Window, a natural limestone arch that sadly collapsed in 2017.

The mild Mediterranean climate of Malta is characterized by hot, dry summers and mild, wet winters. The island enjoys an average of 3,000 hours of sunshine annually, making it a popular destination for sun-seekers. The clear skies and pleasant temperatures during the shoulder seasons attract travelers who want to explore the island's historical sites and outdoor activities without the summer crowds.

# History and Culture

Malta's history is a fascinating mosaic of different civilizations leaving their mark on the islands. One of the earliest known inhabitants of Malta was the prehistoric people who built the megalithic temples, such as Ħaġar Qim and Mnajdra, dating back to around 3600 BC. These temples are considered some of the oldest free-standing structures in the world, predating the Egyptian pyramids and Stonehenge.

The islands were successively ruled by the Phoenicians, Romans, Byzantines, Arabs, and Normans.

A century and a half ago, the Knights of St. John, also known as the Knights Hospitaller, took control of Malta. They built the impressive fortifications that still stand today, such as the fortifications of Valletta, the capital city. The Great Siege of Malta in 1565, when the Knights successfully defended the island against the Ottoman Empire, is a pivotal event in Maltese history and a symbol of their resilience.

Malta's strategic location led to periods of foreign dominion. In the 19th century, it became a British colony, which lasted until it gained independence in 1964. Malta separated from the Commonwealth of Nations in 1974 and became a republic. The legacy of British rule is still evident in aspects of Maltese society, including the use of the English language as one of the official languages alongside Maltese.

History and Culture

Malta's history is a captivating tapestry woven with threads of ancient civilizations, empires, and the resilience of its people. One of the earliest known inhabitants of Malta were the prehistoric people who built the megalithic temples, such as Ħaġar Qim and Mnajdra, dating back to around 3600 BC. These temples are some of the oldest free-standing structures globally, predating even the Egyptian pyramids and Stonehenge.

The archipelago has seen the rise and fall of various empires, from the Phoenicians, Romans, Byzantines, and Arabs to the Normans. A century and a half ago, the Knights of St. John, also known as the Knights Hospitaller, left an indelible mark on Malta. They fortified the island, erecting impressive structures like the fortifications of Valletta, the capital city. The Great Siege of Malta in 1565, when the Knights successfully defended the island against the Ottoman Empire, remains a defining moment in Maltese history.

Malta's cultural tapestry reflects this diverse history. The Maltese language, a unique Semitic language with influences from Latin, Italian, Arabic, and English, is a testament to the nation's historical journey. The Maltese are known for their warm hospitality, and their cultural festivals, such as the Feast of St. George and Carnival, offer vibrant glimpses into their way of life.

Religious festivals, particularly those tied to Catholicism, hold a significant place in Maltese culture. The annual feast of St. Paul's Shipwreck in February is an impressive celebration featuring processions, fireworks, and religious devotion.

Malta's vibrant contemporary arts scene includes theater, film, and literature. The Valletta Film Festival has gained international recognition, and the island has produced talented writers and filmmakers. The iconic film noir, "The Maltese

Falcon," is named after Malta and features Hollywood stars.

## Culture and Language

The Maltese language, a unique Semitic language written in the Latin script, reflects the island's diverse heritage. The linguistic influence of the various civilizations that have shaped Malta is evident in the Maltese vocabulary, making it a linguistic testament to the nation's historical journey.

Malta's culture is a delightful fusion of Mediterranean and European influences. The arts, cuisine, and architecture reflect the island's rich history. Traditional Maltese music and dance, including the lively "Għana" folk music and the "Maltese Cross" dance, are integral to the cultural fabric.

The Maltese are known for their warm hospitality, and their cultural festivals, including the Feast of St. George and Carnival, provide vibrant glimpses into their way of life. Religious festivals, particularly those related to Catholicism, are deeply rooted in Maltese culture. The annual feast of St. Paul's Shipwreck in February is a grand celebration that showcases elaborate processions, fireworks, and religious devotion.

Malta's vibrant contemporary arts scene includes theater, film, and literature. The Valletta Film Festival has gained international recognition, and the island has produced talented writers and filmmakers. Notably, the Maltese Falcon, a classic film noir, was named after Malta and featured iconic Hollywood stars.

**Tourism and Economy**

Tourism plays a vital role in Malta's economy. The country's remarkable history, combined with its stunning natural beauty and warm hospitality, make it an appealing destination for travelers from around the world. Valletta, Malta's capital city, is a UNESCO World Heritage site, and its well-preserved historical sites, such as St. John's Co-Cathedral, draw countless visitors.

Malta's economic development extends beyond tourism. The country has established itself as a hub for the financial services sector and online gaming. The gaming industry, in particular, has experienced significant growth, earning Malta the moniker "The Silicon Valley of iGaming."

Malta is also a member of the European Union, which has opened up opportunities for trade and investment. The country's strategic location has made it a transshipment hub for maritime trade, contributing to its economic resilience.

In recent years, Malta has made significant strides in sustainability and renewable energy, including the development of solar and wind power projects. These initiatives are aligned with Malta's commitment to environmental conservation and its aspirations to be a greener nation.

Cuisine and Gastronomy

Maltese cuisine is a delectable reflection of the island's diverse heritage. The Maltese have perfected the art of combining fresh Mediterranean ingredients with flavors influenced by their historical interactions. Local seafood is a staple, and dishes like "Lampuki Pie" (fish pie) and "Fenkata" (rabbit stew) are Maltese favorites.

A popular snack is the "Pastizz," a flaky pastry filled with ricotta or peas, enjoyed with a cup of tea or a glass of "Kinnie," a local carbonated soft drink. "Ftira," a traditional Maltese bread, is the base for the beloved "ħobż biż-żejt" (bread with oil), typically served with tomatoes, capers, olives, and tuna.

The Maltese sweet tooth is satisfied with desserts like "Imqaret" (date pastries) and "Cannoli," filled with sweet ricotta cream. The local liqueur, "Bajtra," made from prickly pears, is a unique and delicious way to round off a Maltese meal.

Malta, with its rich history, unique language, and vibrant culture, is a hidden gem in the Mediterranean. Its warm hospitality, stunning natural beauty, and diverse cuisine make it an ideal destination for travelers seeking an immersive experience. Whether you are drawn to its ancient temples, fortified cities, or picturesque beaches, Malta's charm is sure to captivate your heart. As this introduction has only scratched the surface of all that Malta has to offer, a visit to the Maltese islands will undoubtedly unveil a wealth of experiences waiting to be discovered.

## Malta's population

Malta is a small island nation located in the Mediterranean Sea, known for its rich history, stunning landscapes, and a unique blend of cultural influences. With a population of approximately 514,564 people as of my last knowledge update in November 2023, Malta is one of the most densely populated countries in the world. In this article, we will explore the demographic composition of Malta, its religious practices, and the cultural significance of religion on the island.

Population of Malta:
Malta's population has experienced significant growth over the years, primarily due to natural increase and immigration. The Maltese people are

renowned for their warmth and hospitality, and the population is known for its multiculturalism. This is due to Malta's strategic location in the Mediterranean, which has historically made it a melting pot of different cultures and traditions.

Demographic Composition:
The Maltese population is predominantly of Maltese ethnicity, and the Maltese language is the official language of the country. Maltese people are known for their strong family ties and traditions, and family is considered the cornerstone of Maltese society. In addition to the Maltese, there are also various minority groups in Malta, including British expatriates and a growing number of immigrants from various countries.

Immigration and Emigration:
Migration has played a crucial role in shaping Malta's population. Historically, many Maltese people emigrated in search of better economic opportunities, especially to the United States and Australia. However, in recent years, Malta has experienced an influx of immigrants, primarily from North Africa and the Middle East, seeking refuge and employment. This has brought new cultural influences and religious diversity to the island.

# Religious Practices in Malta

Religion holds a significant place in the lives of the Maltese people. The Constitution of Malta establishes Roman Catholicism as the state religion and provides for freedom of religion for all citizens. The overwhelming majority of the population, around 98% as of my last update, identifies as Roman Catholic. The Maltese are known for their strong religious convictions and adherence to Catholic traditions.

Catholic Festivals and Traditions:
The Maltese calendar is punctuated by various Catholic festivals and traditions, which play a central role in the lives of the people. Some of the most significant religious events in Malta include Easter and Christmas, celebrated with great fervor and pageantry. The Feast of St. John (San Ġwann) is another notable religious celebration, marked with fireworks, processions, and traditional music.

Churches and Cathedrals:
Malta is dotted with beautiful churches and cathedrals, each with its unique history and architecture. The St. John's Co-Cathedral in Valletta is a UNESCO World Heritage Site and a significant religious landmark. It is adorned with intricate Baroque art, including the famous painting "The Beheading of Saint John the Baptist" by Caravaggio. Many Maltese towns and villages have

their parish churches, and they serve as the focal point for local religious life.

Religious Education:
Religious education is an integral part of the Maltese curriculum. Students in Maltese schools receive religious instruction, mainly in the Catholic faith, which is taught in both primary and secondary education. This reflects the strong influence of religion on the educational system and the broader culture.

Religious Tolerance:
Despite the overwhelming Catholic majority, Malta is generally tolerant of other religious beliefs. Religious and spiritual freedom are guaranteed under the Constitution. Various religious denominations, such as Anglicans, Orthodox Christians, Muslims, and others, have places of worship in Malta. This diversity is more pronounced in recent years due to the influx of immigrants from different religious backgrounds.

Challenges and Changes:
While the Maltese population has historically been deeply rooted in Catholicism, there have been some shifts in recent years. Like many Western countries, Malta has seen a decline in church attendance and religious vocations. Secularization and changing societal attitudes are influencing the younger generation's religious beliefs and practices.

Malta's population is marked by its rich cultural diversity and strong ties to the Roman Catholic faith. Religion plays a central role in the lives of the Maltese people, with Catholic traditions and celebrations being deeply ingrained in their cultural identity. However, the country also experiences the challenges of modernization, with changing demographics and attitudes affecting religious practices. Malta's unique blend of history, religion, and multiculturalism continues to shape its dynamic and evolving population.

Chapter One

# Planning Your Trip

## When to Visit Malta

Malta is a beautiful Mediterranean island nation known for its rich history, stunning landscapes, and vibrant culture. When planning your trip to Malta, the timing of your visit can greatly influence your experience. Here's a guide on when to visit Malta:

Spring (March to May): Spring is a fantastic time to visit Malta. The weather starts to warm up, and the island becomes lush and green with blooming flowers. The temperatures are comfortable, ranging from 15°C to 20°C (59°F to 68°F), making it perfect for exploring the historic sites and enjoying outdoor activities.

Summer (June to August): Summer is the peak tourist season in Malta. The weather is hot and dry, with temperatures often exceeding 30°C (86°F). This is the ideal time for sunbathing, swimming, and enjoying the beautiful beaches. The nightlife is also lively, with various festivals and events taking place.

Autumn (September to November): Autumn is another excellent time to visit Malta. The weather remains pleasant with temperatures ranging from 20°C to 25°C (68°F to 77°F). It's less crowded compared to summer, and you can still enjoy the beaches, water sports, and outdoor activities. The sea is warm for swimming.

Winter (December to February): While winters in Malta are mild compared to many other European destinations, it's the off-season for tourism. The temperatures typically range from 10°C to 15°C (50°F to 59°F). If you prefer a quieter, more budget-friendly visit and are interested in exploring historical sites without the crowds, this is a good time to go. Keep in mind that some attractions and restaurants may have limited hours during the winter months.

In summary, the best time to visit Malta depends on your preferences. If you enjoy warm weather, vibrant festivals, and a lively atmosphere, summer is the way to go. Spring and autumn offer pleasant weather with fewer crowds, making them great choices for a more relaxed experience. Winter can be a peaceful time to explore the island's history and natural beauty, but be prepared for cooler temperatures and shorter days.

# Visa and Entry Requirements

Visa and entry requirements for Malta vary depending on your nationality, the purpose of your visit, and the duration of your stay. Here's an elaborate overview of the visa and entry requirements for Malta:

1. Schengen Area: Malta is part of the Schengen Area, which allows for passport-free travel between member countries. If you are a citizen of a Schengen Area country, you can enter Malta without a visa and stay for up to 90 days within a 180-day period. These countries include most European Union (EU) nations, such as France, Germany, Italy, and Spain.

2. Non-Schengen Area Countries: If you are a citizen of a non-Schengen Area country, including the United States, Canada, Australia, and many others, you can also enter Malta for short stays of up to 90 days within a 180-day period without a visa.

3. Visa-Exempt Countries: Malta has a list of visa-exempt countries whose citizens can enter Malta for short visits without a visa. However, the exact list and conditions can change, so it's essential to check with the Maltese embassy or

consulate in your home country or the official Maltese government website for the most up-to-date information.

4. Long-Term Stays: If you plan to stay in Malta for more than 90 days or for purposes such as work, study, or family reunification, you will need to apply for a long-term visa or residence permit. The type of visa or permit you need will depend on the specific circumstances of your stay.

5. Visa Application: To apply for a visa or residence permit, you'll typically need to visit the nearest Maltese embassy or consulate in your home country. You will be required to submit various documents, including a visa application form, passport-sized photos, proof of accommodation, travel insurance, proof of financial means, and a valid passport.

6. Schengen Visa: If you plan to visit other Schengen countries in addition to Malta, you can apply for a Schengen visa at a Maltese consulate or embassy. This visa allows you to travel to all Schengen countries during your stay.

7. Visa Processing Time: Visa processing times may vary, so it's advisable to apply well in advance of your intended travel dates. Be prepared for potential interviews or additional documentation requests during the application process.

8. Entry and Exit Requirements: Ensure that your passport is valid for at least six months beyond your intended departure date from Malta. You may also be asked for proof of a return ticket and accommodation during your stay.

9. Travel Insurance: It's recommended to have travel insurance that covers medical expenses for the duration of your stay in Malta.

Always check the most recent visa and entry requirements, as they can change due to international agreements or changes in Maltese law. It's advisable to contact the Maltese embassy or consulate in your home country or refer to the official Maltese government website for the latest information to ensure a smooth and trouble-free entry into Malta.

## Currency and Budgeting

Understanding the currency and budgeting for your trip to Malta is essential to ensure a smooth and enjoyable travel experience. Here's a guide on the currency, cost of living, and budgeting for your stay in Malta:

**Currency:**

Malta's official currency is the Euro (€), and it is used throughout the country. It's recommended to have some Euros with you upon arrival, and you can obtain them from ATMs or currency exchange offices at the airport or in major towns.

Cost of Living:

Malta is considered a moderately expensive destination, and the cost of living can vary depending on your choices and preferences. To give you an idea of the estimated costs:

Accommodation: Accommodation costs can vary widely, from budget hostels and guesthouses to luxury hotels. On average, you can expect to spend around €50 to €150 per night, depending on your choice of accommodation.

Dining: Dining out in Malta can be affordable, especially if you opt for local, casual eateries. A meal at a mid-range restaurant may cost around €15 to €30, while a quick street food snack can be as low as €5.

Transportation: Public transportation is reasonably priced in Malta, with a single bus fare costing approximately €2. A seven-day bus pass is also available for around €21. Taxis are more expensive, so consider public transport or car rentals for budget-conscious travelers.

Attractions and Activities: Many historical sites and museums have admission fees, which can range from €5 to €15. Outdoor activities like water sports or boat tours might have higher costs, so plan accordingly.

Groceries: If you prefer self-catering, groceries are relatively affordable. A basic grocery shopping for a week can cost around €30 to €50, depending on your preferences.

Entertainment: Prices for entertainment, such as cinema tickets or a night out, can vary, but expect to spend around €10 to €20 for these activities.

**Budgeting Tips:**

To create a budget for your trip to Malta, consider the following tips:

Research Accommodation: Look for accommodation options that match your budget. Early reservations can frequently result in financial savings.

Use Public Transport: Malta has an efficient bus network that can help you save on transportation costs. Consider buying a bus pass for extended stays.

Plan Your Meals: While dining out is part of the experience, having some meals in local cafes and preparing simple dishes in your accommodation can help control food expenses.

Prioritize Activities: Plan your activities and prioritize the ones you don't want to miss. Budget for entrance fees to attractions and set aside money for tours and experiences.

Exchange Currency Wisely: Compare exchange rates to get the best value for your money. It's also a good idea to inform your bank of your travel plans to avoid any issues with your credit or debit cards.

Lastly, it's a good practice to have a contingency fund for unexpected expenses or emergencies during your trip.

Remember that the actual budget for your Malta trip will depend on your personal preferences, travel style, and the duration of your stay. By carefully planning and budgeting, you can make the most of your time in this beautiful Mediterranean destination without breaking the bank.

# Language and Communication

Language and communication in Malta are essential aspects of your travel experience. Understanding the local languages, communication options, and cultural nuances can greatly enhance your interactions with the Maltese people. Here's an elaborate guide on language and communication in Malta:

**Official Languages:**

Malta has two official languages: *Maltese* and *English*. Both languages play significant roles in daily life and are widely spoken and understood by the local population.

**Maltese**: Maltese is the national language of Malta and is unique to the country. It has Semitic roots and is written in the Latin script. While it might sound intimidating at first, you'll find that many Maltese people are bilingual and can switch between Maltese and English effortlessly.

**English**: English is also an official language and is widely spoken, especially in urban areas, by the majority of the population. This makes Malta a very accessible destination for English-speaking travelers.

**Communication Tips:**

Here are some communication tips to help you navigate language and cultural interactions in Malta:

Greet in Maltese: Learning a few basic Maltese greetings, like "Bongu" (Good morning) or "Lejl it-tajjeb" (Good evening), can be a polite way to start a conversation and show respect for the local culture.

Use English as a Backup: While you may encounter some Maltese people who speak limited English, especially in rural areas, English is widely used for business, tourism, and official purposes. It's recommended to use English for most of your interactions.

Politeness and Courtesy: Maltese people are generally polite and friendly. It's customary to be courteous and use polite phrases, such as "Jekk jogħġbok" (Please) and "Grazzi" (Thank you).

Be Patient: If you do encounter language barriers or communication challenges, patience and a friendly demeanor can go a long way in overcoming them. Maltese people appreciate travelers who make an effort to engage with their culture.

Cultural Sensitivity: Understanding local customs and cultural norms is important. Malta has a Catholic tradition, so it's advisable to be respectful in your attire and behavior, especially when visiting religious sites.

**Local Dialects:**

In addition to standard Maltese and English, you may encounter regional dialects and accents in Malta. Some of the smaller islands and rural areas have their own variations of the Maltese language, which can be quite distinct from the standard Maltese spoken in urban centers.

Signage and Information:

Most signage and information for tourists are available in both Maltese and English. This includes street signs, menus, brochures, and information at tourist sites.

Technology and Internet:

The use of smartphones and the internet is widespread in Malta. You can easily access mobile data and use messaging apps to communicate with locals and navigate the island.

Emergency Numbers:

The emergency number in Malta is 112, which you can call for police, medical assistance, or the fire department.

In summary, while Maltese is the national language, English is the lingua franca for most interactions, making Malta a welcoming destination for English-speaking travelers. Being respectful, polite, and culturally sensitive will help you connect with the locals and make your stay in Malta a more enriching experience.

Chapter Two

# Getting to Malta

## Flights to Malta

Getting to Malta by air is a convenient and popular option for travelers from around the world. Malta International Airport, also known as Luqa Airport, is the only airport in Malta and serves as the primary gateway to the country. Here's an overview of how to get to Malta by flights:

International Flights: Malta International Airport is well-connected with various international airports, making it accessible to travelers from Europe, North Africa, and the Middle East. You can find direct flights to Malta from major cities like London, Paris, Rome, Frankfurt, Istanbul, and many more.

Airlines: Several major airlines operate flights to and from Malta. Some of the prominent carriers serving Malta include Air Malta, Ryanair, easyJet, British Airways, Lufthansa, and Emirates, among others. These airlines offer a range of options in terms of schedules and price points.

Seasonal Variations: Flight availability and prices can vary depending on the season. Malta is a popular summer destination, so flights and accommodation tend to be more expensive during the peak tourist season, which typically runs from June to September. If you're looking for a more budget-friendly trip, consider visiting during the shoulder seasons of spring or autumn.

Flight Duration: The duration of your flight to Malta will depend on your departure location. European flights are relatively short, usually ranging from 2 to 4 hours, while flights from more distant locations can take significantly longer.

Airport Facilities: Malta International Airport is a modern facility with a range of services, including duty-free shops, car rental services, restaurants, and currency exchange counters. It's well-equipped to handle the needs of international travelers.

Visa and Entry Requirements: Ensure that you have the necessary visa or travel documentation based on your nationality and the purpose of your visit. Malta is part of the Schengen Area, which allows for easy travel within participating European countries.

Transportation from the Airport: After your arrival in Malta, you can easily reach your destination by using various transportation options, including taxis, shuttle buses, and car rentals. Public buses also connect the airport to different parts of the island.

COVID-19 Considerations: As of my last knowledge update in January 2022, the travel landscape had been significantly affected by the COVID-19 pandemic. Please check the latest travel advisories, entry requirements, and health and safety protocols before planning your trip, as these guidelines may change.

Accommodation: Ensure you have your accommodation booked in advance, especially during peak tourist seasons, as availability can be limited.

Explore Malta: Once you arrive, make the most of your trip by exploring Malta's beautiful landscapes, historic sites, and vibrant culture. From the ancient city of Mdina to the stunning Blue Grotto, Malta has a lot to offer.

When planning your journey to Malta, it's essential to consider your travel dates, budget, and personal preferences. Whether you're a leisure traveler or on a business trip, the options available for flights to Malta cater to a wide range of needs.

# Transportation within Malta

Transportation within Malta is relatively easy and convenient, making it accessible to both tourists and residents. The small size of the island nation, efficient infrastructure, and diverse modes of transportation all contribute to a hassle-free travel experience. Here's an overview of transportation options within Malta:

Public Bus: Malta has an extensive and well-organized public bus network operated by Malta Public Transport. The buses cover the entire island, including popular tourist destinations and rural areas. Each bus route is color-coded and numbered, and schedules are available online or at bus stops. The bus system is an affordable and eco-friendly way to explore the island. You can purchase tickets on the bus or opt for a Tallinja card for discounted fares.

Ferries: Malta is an archipelago, and there are several ferry services that connect the main island of Malta with its sister islands, Gozo and Comino. These ferries are a scenic way to travel between islands and provide breathtaking views of the Mediterranean Sea. The Gozo Channel ferry service is the primary operator, running between Cirkewwa in Malta and Mgarr in Gozo.

Taxis: Taxis are readily available in Malta and are a convenient way to get around, especially for shorter journeys or when you want to reach destinations not easily accessible by public transportation. Taxis can be reserved in advance or called upon the street. It's a more expensive option compared to buses, but it offers more privacy and comfort.

Car Rentals: Renting a car is a popular choice for travelers who want the flexibility to explore Malta at their own pace. Many international car rental agencies have offices at Malta International Airport, and you can also find local rental companies. Malta's road network is well-maintained, and driving is on the left side of the road. However, parking can be challenging in some areas, especially in the more densely populated parts of the island.

Bicycles and Scooters: Malta's small size and relatively flat terrain make it ideal for cycling. Some areas have dedicated bike lanes, and you can rent bicycles at various locations. Scooter rentals are also available, providing an efficient way to maneuver through traffic and explore the island's nooks and crannies.

Walking: Malta's towns and cities are pedestrian-friendly, and walking is a pleasant way to explore urban areas, visit historic sites, and enjoy the Mediterranean ambiance. Strolling through the charming streets of Valletta, Mdina, or the Three Cities is a must for any visitor.

Hop-On-Hop-Off Buses: Malta offers hop-on-hop-off bus tours that take you to the island's top tourist attractions, allowing you to explore at your own pace. These tours provide informative commentary and are a convenient way to see the sights.

Electric Cabs: In an effort to reduce pollution, electric cabs have become more popular in Malta, particularly in the Valletta area. These cabs offer a sustainable and eco-friendly mode of transportation.

Cable Cars: The Blue Grotto in Malta can be reached via cable car, offering a unique way to access this popular tourist site. The cable car ride provides stunning views of the coastline.

Travel Cards: If you plan to use public transportation extensively, consider purchasing a travel card such as the Tallinja card, which offers discounted fares for buses and ferries, or the Valletta Card, which includes unlimited travel on public transport in the Valletta area and free admission to many museums and sites.

Transportation within Malta is generally reliable and offers a range of options to suit different preferences and budgets. Whether you choose to use the efficient bus system, rent a car to explore at your own pace, or simply walk around the charming streets, you'll have no trouble getting around and enjoying all that Malta has to offer.

# Airport Information

Airport information is vital for travelers, whether you're planning a trip to a new destination or just curious about the facilities and services available at a particular airport. Here's an overview of airport information, covering the key aspects you should be aware of when using an airport, with a focus on Malta International Airport as an example:

Location: Malta International Airport, also known as Luqa Airport, is the primary international gateway to the Maltese Islands. It is located in Luqa, about 5 kilometers southwest of the capital city, Valletta. The airport's coordinates are 35.8497° N latitude and 14.4844° E longitude.

**Facilities and Services:**

Terminals: Malta International Airport has one main terminal building, which is modern and well-maintained.
Check-In: The airport provides a range of check-in options, including self-check-in kiosks and traditional check-in counters for various airlines.

Security and Immigration: Standard security and immigration procedures are in place to ensure the safety and efficiency of your journey.

Baggage Handling: Baggage handling facilities are available, and the airport offers services for lost or delayed baggage.

Shops and Duty-Free: You'll find a variety of shops, including duty-free outlets, selling a wide range of products, from souvenirs to luxury items.

Restaurants and Cafes: Several dining options are available, offering local and international cuisine, as well as snacks and beverages.

Currency Exchange: Currency exchange counters and ATMs are located within the terminal for your convenience.

Car Rental Services: Various car rental companies have offices at the airport, making it easy to rent a vehicle for your stay.

Lounges: The airport has VIP and business lounges, where you can relax and enjoy complimentary services if you have access through your ticket class or loyalty program.

Disabled and Special Needs Services: Malta International Airport is equipped to assist passengers with disabilities and special needs. Services include wheelchair assistance and accessible facilities.

Parking: The airport has both short-term and long-term parking areas for travelers who need to leave their vehicles at the airport.

**Transportation to and from the Airport:**

Taxis: Taxis are readily available at the airport, providing a convenient way to reach your destination.
Shuttle Buses: Shuttle services operate to various locations on the island, offering shared transportation options.
Public Buses: Malta Public Transport buses connect the airport to different parts of the island, making it an economical choice.
Car Rentals: Car rental agencies have counters at the airport, allowing you to pick up a vehicle upon arrival.
Ferries: If you plan to visit the sister islands of Gozo and Comino, you can take a ferry from the nearby Cirkewwa terminal.
COVID-19 Protocols: Depending on the global and local COVID-19 situation, airports may have specific health and safety protocols in place. These can include requirements for testing, mask-wearing, and social distancing. It's essential to check the latest guidelines and requirements before your journey.

Flight Information: The airport provides real-time flight information, including departure and arrival times, gate information, and baggage claim details. You can check this information on the airport's website or through information boards within the terminal.

Visa and Passport Requirements: Ensure that you have the necessary visas and travel documentation required for your destination. Malta is part of the Schengen Area, so EU and EFTA citizens typically don't require a visa for short visits.

Understanding the facilities, services, and logistics of an airport, such as Malta International Airport, can make your journey smoother and more enjoyable. It's always a good practice to check with the specific airport's website for the most up-to-date information and to plan your travel accordingly.

# Public Transportation

Public transportation plays a critical role in the daily lives of people worldwide, offering an efficient, cost-effective, and sustainable means of getting around cities and regions. Here's an elaborate overview of public transportation, covering the key aspects and benefits of this essential service:

**Modes of Public Transportation:**

Bus Transportation:

Buses are one of the most common and versatile forms of public transportation, serving both urban and rural areas. They are especially prevalent in cities and towns, providing comprehensive coverage.

Benefits: Buses are cost-effective, accessible, and can navigate various routes, making them a convenient option for daily commuting. They reduce traffic congestion and pollution, contributing to environmental sustainability.

Subway/Metro Systems:

Subways and metro systems are prevalent in many major cities around the world. These underground or elevated rail networks are known for their speed and efficiency.

Benefits: Subways offer rapid transit, reducing travel time and easing congestion on city streets. They are energy-efficient and often a preferred mode of transportation during rush hours.

Trams and Light Rail:

Trams and light rail systems provide public transportation on dedicated tracks within urban areas. They work especially well over small distances.

Benefits: Trams are known for their reliability and environmental friendliness. They can help revitalize urban areas and stimulate local economies.

Commuter Trains:

Commuter trains are designed for passengers traveling between cities and suburbs. They connect regions and often provide a more comfortable and spacious travel experience.
Benefits: Commuter trains are ideal for long-distance commuting, and they reduce the number of vehicles on highways, alleviating traffic congestion.

Ferries and Water Taxis:

In regions with water bodies, ferries and water taxis are common modes of public transportation. They connect islands, coastal areas, and waterfront districts.
Benefits: Water transportation is not only scenic but also efficient for reaching destinations that are otherwise hard to access by road.

## Advantages of Public Transportation:

Economic Benefits:

Taking public transit can be less expensive than buying and maintaining a private car. It reduces individual fuel and maintenance costs.
It stimulates the local economy by creating jobs in transportation and related industries.


Environmental Benefits:

In general, using public transit is more environmentally beneficial than driving a private car.. It reduces air pollution, greenhouse gas emissions, and overall carbon footprint.
Using fewer vehicles on the road contributes to improved air quality and less traffic congestion.

Reduced Traffic Congestion:

Public transportation systems help decongest roads and highways, leading to smoother traffic flow and shorter commute times for everyone.
Fewer cars on the road also mean reduced stress for drivers and fewer accidents.

Accessibility and Inclusivity:

Public transportation is essential for people who cannot drive, such as the elderly, disabled, and those without access to private vehicles.
It promotes social inclusion by providing affordable transportation options for all.

Urban Planning and Land Use:

Well-designed public transportation systems influence urban development and reduce urban sprawl.
They promote compact, walkable communities with easy access to essential services and amenities.

Reduced Energy Consumption:

Public transportation is more energy-efficient, as it carries multiple passengers in a single vehicle.
It lowers the need for fossil fuels in general.

Challenges and Considerations:

Funding and Investment: Developing and maintaining public transportation systems require significant financial investments. Governments often subsidize these services to keep them affordable.

Infrastructure and Expansion: Expanding and upgrading public transportation networks can be challenging due to limited space and the need for extensive infrastructure development.

Service Reliability: Consistency and reliability in scheduling and service quality are essential for building public trust and encouraging ridership.

Safety and Security: Ensuring the safety and security of passengers is a priority, especially during late-night or off-peak hours.

Technological Advancements: The integration of modern technology, such as real-time tracking and electronic ticketing, is essential to improving the convenience of public transportation.

Public transportation is a cornerstone of sustainable, efficient, and accessible urban and regional development. It plays a significant role in reducing the environmental impact of transportation, improving the quality of life in cities, and providing affordable mobility options for diverse populations. Whether you're a daily commuter or a traveler exploring a new city, understanding and utilizing public transportation can have numerous personal and societal benefits.

# Chapter Three

# Accommodation

## Types of Accommodation

Accommodation in Malta offers a diverse range of options to suit various preferences and budgets. Here's a tip on the types of accommodation you can find in Malta:

Hotels: Malta boasts a wide selection of hotels, ranging from luxurious five-star resorts to budget-friendly options. These hotels provide various amenities, including restaurants, bars, pools, and fitness centers. Many are located in popular tourist areas like Valletta, St. Julian's, and Sliema.

Apartments: Self-catering apartments are popular among tourists who prefer more independence and space. You can find furnished apartments in different sizes, often with fully equipped kitchens, making them ideal for longer stays. Many apartments are located in residential areas, offering a taste of local life.

Hostels: If you're traveling on a tight budget, hostels in Malta offer affordable dormitory-style accommodations. These are great for backpackers and solo travelers, providing a social atmosphere and the chance to meet fellow travelers. Private rooms are sometimes available in hostels as well.

Guesthouses and B&Bs: Malta has numerous guesthouses and bed-and-breakfasts, particularly in historic towns like Mdina and Rabat. These quaint accommodations offer a more intimate and personalized experience, often in charming historic buildings.

Farmhouses and Villas: For a unique and luxurious experience, consider renting a traditional Maltese farmhouse or a villa, especially if you're traveling with a group. These properties often come with private pools and stunning views of the Mediterranean.

Rural and Eco-Accommodations: Malta's countryside offers eco-friendly options, such as eco-lodges and farm stays. These accommodations focus on sustainability and allow you to connect with nature while enjoying the serene Maltese landscapes.

Camping and Glamping: Camping is possible in designated areas, and some campsites even offer glamping (glamorous camping) facilities with more comfortable amenities. It's a great way to immerse yourself in the natural beauty of Malta.

Timeshares and Vacation Rentals: Some travelers opt for timeshares or vacation rentals, which can be found through various platforms. These offer a home-like atmosphere and are suitable for those looking for extended stays.

Boat Stays: Malta's stunning coastline and harbors make it a unique destination for boat accommodations. You can rent a boat or book a stay on a houseboat, providing a one-of-a-kind experience on the water.

Each type of accommodation in Malta has its own advantages and caters to different tastes and budgets. Whether you're looking for a relaxing beachfront retreat, a cultural city stay, or an adventurous rural experience, you'll find suitable options in this picturesque Mediterranean archipelago.

# Recommended Hotels and Resorts

Malta offers a diverse array of hotels and resorts to cater to various tastes and preferences. Here are some recommended options, each with its own unique charm:

The Phoenicia Malta (Valletta): This iconic 5-star hotel is situated in the heart of Valletta, the capital city of Malta. The Phoenicia boasts a rich history and elegant colonial-style architecture. Its lush gardens, exceptional dining options, and stunning views of the city and the Grand Harbour make it a top choice for luxury travelers.

Corinthia Palace Hotel & Spa (Attard): If you're seeking a tranquil oasis, the Corinthia Palace is an excellent choice. Nestled in the peaceful village of Attard, it features beautifully landscaped gardens, a renowned spa, and a selection of restaurants. It's conveniently located for exploring the historic town of Mdina.

The Westin Dragonara Resort (St. Julian's): Overlooking the Mediterranean Sea, The Westin Dragonara Resort is a 5-star haven in the bustling town of St. Julian's. It offers direct access to the sea, multiple swimming pools, and a variety of dining options. The lively nightlife of Paceville is within walking distance.

Hotel Juliani (St. Julian's): For a boutique experience, consider Hotel Juliani. This charming hotel combines modern design with a welcoming atmosphere. It's situated on the St. Julian's waterfront and offers breathtaking sea views from its stylish rooms and rooftop terrace.

Radisson Blu Resort & Spa (Golden Bay): If you're a beach lover, the Radisson Blu at Golden Bay is an ideal choice. This 5-star resort sits on one of Malta's most beautiful sandy beaches and offers fantastic facilities, including an expansive pool, spa, and excellent dining options.

Grand Hotel Excelsior (Valletta): With a prime location along the Valletta waterfront, the Grand Hotel Excelsior offers a luxurious experience. It features a private beach club, outdoor pool, and spectacular views of the historic city. It's also within walking distance of Valletta's main attractions.

InterContinental Malta (St. George's Bay): This modern and stylish 5-star hotel is located in St. George's Bay, near the vibrant entertainment district of St. Julian's. The InterContinental offers a variety of restaurants, a spa, and direct access to the beach.

Hilton Malta (St. Julian's): Overlooking the Portomaso Marina, the Hilton Malta is a lavish hotel known for its spacious rooms, fantastic spa, and several dining options. It's also in close proximity to the lively St. Julian's area.

Kempinski Hotel San Lawrenz (Gozo): If you're planning to explore Gozo, the Kempinski Hotel San Lawrenz is a top choice. This 5-star resort offers a peaceful countryside setting, a luxurious spa, and proximity to the island's key attractions.

Palazzo Prince d'Orange (Valletta): For a unique boutique experience, consider this historic 17th-century palazzo turned boutique hotel. It's located in the heart of Valletta and offers beautifully restored rooms with an old-world charm.

These recommended hotels and resorts cater to a range of preferences, from historic elegance to beachfront luxury and modern sophistication. Regardless of your choice, you can expect warm Maltese hospitality and a memorable stay on this beautiful Mediterranean island.

# Hostels and Guesthouses

For travelers seeking budget-friendly and more intimate accommodations in Malta, hostels and guesthouses provide excellent options. Here's an elaboration on these choices:

**Hostels**:

Hostel Malti (St. Julian's): This trendy and vibrant hostel is located in the heart of St. Julian's, a popular nightlife area. Hostel Malti offers affordable dormitory-style rooms, a communal kitchen, and a lively social atmosphere. It's perfect for young backpackers and those looking to meet fellow travelers.

Hostel Jones (Sliema): Known for its eco-friendly initiatives and creative design, Hostel Jones in Sliema provides a unique hostel experience. They offer both dorms and private rooms, a communal kitchen, and a communal garden where they host events and activities.

Sant' Angelo Hostel (Rabat): If you prefer a quieter and historic setting, Sant' Angelo Hostel in Rabat, near the medieval city of Mdina, is a charming choice. It's set in a traditional Maltese townhouse and provides a more relaxed atmosphere.

Marco Polo Hostel (Valletta): This budget-friendly hostel is located right in Valletta, the capital of Malta. It offers dormitory-style accommodations, a cozy lounge area, and a shared kitchen. It's ideal for exploring the historic city on foot.

**Guesthouses and B&Bs:**

The Point Boutique Hotel (Marsaxlokk): The Point offers a personalized boutique experience in the picturesque fishing village of Marsaxlokk. This guesthouse features comfortable rooms, a terrace with sea views, and a restaurant serving fresh seafood.

190 St. George's (St. Julian's): This family-run guesthouse is set in a historic townhouse in St. Julian's. It offers a cozy and homely atmosphere, with tastefully decorated rooms and a lovely courtyard. It's a short walk from the bustling nightlife of Paceville.

Loggia Mariposa (Mdina): Located within the ancient walled city of Mdina, Loggia Mariposa offers an enchanting experience. This historic building features well-appointed guestrooms and a peaceful courtyard. It feels like a trip through time to stay here.

Ta' Bertu Host Family Bed & Breakfast (Mġarr): If you're looking for an authentic and welcoming experience, consider a stay at this family-run B&B in the village of Mġarr on Gozo. The hosts provide warm Maltese hospitality and can introduce you to the local culture.

Palazzo Prince d'Orange (Valletta): While previously mentioned in the hotel section, this 17th-century palazzo also offers a few guestrooms. It's an excellent choice if you want a more boutique and intimate stay within Valletta's historic core.

Hostels and guesthouses in Malta provide affordable and personalized lodging options, allowing you to experience the island's culture and charm in a more immersive way. Whether you opt for the social vibes of a hostel or the warmth of a guesthouse, you're sure to find a cozy and budget-friendly place to call home during your visit to Malta.

# Vacation Rentals

Vacation rentals in Malta offer a wonderful way to experience the destination like a local, providing you with more space, privacy, and the flexibility to tailor your stay to your preferences. Here's an elaborate look at vacation rentals in Malta:

Apartments: Vacation apartments are widely available across Malta, and they range from compact studios to spacious penthouses. These rentals often come with fully equipped kitchens, making it convenient for self-catering. You can find apartments in various parts of the island, including popular areas like Valletta, Sliema, and St. Julian's, offering both urban and seaside living options.

Villas: If you're traveling with a group or desire a more secluded and luxurious experience, renting a villa in Malta is an excellent choice. Villas can be found in both urban and rural settings, with many offering private pools, gardens, and stunning sea views. Gozo, Malta's sister island, is particularly known for its beautiful villa rentals.

Farmhouses: In rural areas of Malta and Gozo, you can discover traditional Maltese farmhouses available for rent. These properties provide a unique blend of historic charm and modern amenities. They often feature courtyards, swimming pools, and panoramic countryside views, creating a serene and picturesque atmosphere.

Townhouses: Malta is dotted with charming townhouses that offer a blend of historic architecture and contemporary comforts. Townhouse vacation rentals are typically found in the heart of old towns and villages like Rabat and Marsaxlokk, allowing you to immerse yourself in the local culture.

Cottages: For a cozy and authentic experience, consider renting a Maltese cottage. These properties are often nestled in scenic countryside settings, providing a peaceful escape from the bustling city life. They are especially popular for travelers seeking a romantic retreat.

Historic Residences: Malta is home to many historic residences and palazzos that have been converted into vacation rentals. Staying in one of these properties offers a taste of the island's rich heritage and architectural splendor.

Seaside Houses: If you're a beach enthusiast, consider a vacation rental near the coast. These properties often come with direct access to the sea, allowing you to enjoy the beautiful Mediterranean waters just steps from your doorstep.

Lighthouse Accommodations: For a truly unique experience, you can even find vacation rentals in historic lighthouses, offering unparalleled sea views and an extraordinary atmosphere.

Boat Rentals: Malta's coastal location makes it a great destination for boat rentals. You can rent sailboats, catamarans, or even houseboats, allowing you to explore the Maltese coastline and anchor at scenic spots.

Vacation rentals in Malta cater to a wide range of travelers, from families and groups to couples and solo adventurers. They provide a flexible and immersive way to enjoy the island, allowing you to live like a local and create your own unforgettable experiences while enjoying the natural beauty, culture, and history of Malta.

Chapter Four

# Exploring Malta's island top attractions

Malta is a beautiful island with plenty of top attractions to explore. Here are some of the must-visit places and activities:

Valletta: Malta's capital city is a UNESCO World Heritage site known for its historic architecture, museums, and stunning views from the Upper Barrakka Gardens.

Mdina: This ancient walled city is often called the "Silent City" and is full of narrow streets and medieval charm.

Blue Grotto: Take a boat tour to this series of caves and marvel at the crystal-clear blue waters and unique rock formations.

Gozo: A short ferry ride away, Gozo offers beautiful beaches, the Azure Window (a natural rock arch), and the historic Citadel.

Comino: Visit the tiny island of Comino, known for its Blue Lagoon with its incredibly clear waters, perfect for swimming and snorkeling.

Hagar Qim and Mnajdra Temples: Explore these ancient megalithic temples, which are some of the oldest free-standing structures in the world.

St. John's Co-Cathedral: Admire the ornate interior of this Baroque cathedral in Valletta, known for its impressive artwork.

Marsaxlokk: A picturesque fishing village with colorful boats and a vibrant Sunday fish market.

The Hypogeum: An underground prehistoric temple and burial site, a UNESCO World Heritage site.

Dingli Cliffs: Enjoy breathtaking views from the highest point on the island, Dingli Cliffs.

Popeye Village: Visit the movie set turned theme park of the 1980 film "Popeye."

Diving and Snorkeling: Malta offers fantastic underwater experiences with numerous wrecks, caves, and marine life to explore.

Local Cuisine: Savor Maltese dishes like pastizzi (pastries filled with cheese or peas), rabbit stew, and ftira (local bread).

Festivals: Check the local calendar for traditional Maltese festivals, such as the feasts of various saints celebrated with colorful processions and fireworks.

Malta has a rich history and a mix of natural and cultural attractions, making it a great destination for travelers. Don't forget to take your time and enjoy the Mediterranean climate and hospitality.

# Top tourist cities to stay in Malta

Malta offers several fantastic cities and towns for tourists to stay in, each with its own unique charm and attractions. Here are some of the top tourist cities to consider when visiting Malta:

Valletta: Malta's capital city, Valletta, is a UNESCO World Heritage site and a hub of history, culture, and stunning architecture. It offers a wide range of accommodations, including boutique hotels and luxury options.

St. Julian's: Known for its vibrant nightlife and entertainment, St. Julian's is a popular choice for tourists looking to enjoy the lively side of Malta. It's also home to the picturesque Spinola Bay.

Sliema: Located right next to St. Julian's, Sliema is a bustling coastal town with a beautiful promenade, shopping opportunities, and various hotels and apartments.

Mdina: This ancient walled city, often referred to as the "Silent City," offers a unique and tranquil experience. While there are fewer accommodations within Mdina itself, there are options in the nearby town of Rabat.

Birgu (Vittoriosa), Senglea (Isla), and Cospicua (Bormla): These three cities make up the Three Cities area and are rich in history, with narrow streets, fortifications, and waterfront views. They offer a quieter and more authentic Maltese experience.

Mellieha: Located in the north of Malta, Mellieha is known for its sandy beaches and natural beauty. It's an excellent choice for families and those seeking a more relaxed atmosphere.

Gozo (Island): While not a city, Gozo is Malta's sister island and offers a serene and rustic experience. You can find accommodations in towns like Victoria (Rabat), Xlendi, and Marsalforn.

Marsaxlokk: A charming fishing village in the south of Malta, known for its colorful boats and a lively Sunday fish market. It's a great place to experience traditional Maltese life.

Xlendi: A picturesque bay on the island of Gozo, Xlendi is popular for its scenic cliffs, clear waters, and seafood restaurants.

Comino (Island): Although tiny, Comino is a popular day trip destination from Malta. It's known for the Blue Lagoon and offers a tranquil escape from the crowds.

These cities and towns in Malta cater to a variety of preferences, from historical and cultural experiences to beachside relaxation and vibrant nightlife. Your decision will be based on the kind of experience you're looking for as well as your interests.

# Historical Sites and Museums

Valletta: Malta's capital city, Valletta, is a treasure trove of historical sites. Explore St. John's Co-Cathedral, known for its opulent Baroque interior, and the Grand Master's Palace. The

National Museum of Archaeology in Valletta houses a remarkable collection of prehistoric artifacts.

Mdina: The ancient walled city of Mdina is a living museum. Walk along its narrow, winding streets and visit the Mdina Cathedral and the Palazzo Falson Historic House Museum.

Hagar Qim and Mnajdra Temples: These megalithic temples, dating back over 5,000 years, are a UNESCO World Heritage site. They offer a fascinating glimpse into Malta's prehistoric past.

The Hypogeum: This underground temple and burial site is a must-visit. It's one of the most significant archaeological sites in Malta and provides insights into the island's ancient civilization.

National War Museum: Housed in Fort St. Elmo in Valletta, this museum showcases Malta's military history, including artifacts from World War II.

Gozo Citadel: In the town of Victoria (Rabat) on Gozo, you can explore the medieval walls and cathedral within the Citadel, offering panoramic views of the island.

# Beaches and Coastal Activities

Golden Bay: This sandy beach is perfect for sunbathing and swimming. It's known for its golden sand and clear waters.

Mellieha Bay: Located in the north of Malta, Mellieha Bay is the island's largest sandy beach, making it great for families and water sports.

Blue Grotto: Take a boat tour to explore the stunning sea caves and crystal-clear waters. For divers and snorkelers, it's a heaven.

Ramla Bay, Gozo: Known for its reddish-gold sand, Ramla Bay is one of the most scenic beaches on Gozo.

Dwejra Bay, Gozo: Visit the Inland Sea, the Blue Hole, and the collapsed Azure Window, a mecca for divers.

Comino's Blue Lagoon: This shallow, azure-water lagoon is a snorkeler's dream and a stunning spot for sunbathing and swimming.

# Rural and Natural Attractions

Dingli Cliffs: These cliffs offer spectacular views of the Mediterranean Sea and are perfect for a leisurely walk or hike.

Gozo's Inland Sea: It's a unique coastal lagoon connected to the sea through a natural arch. Take a boat trip and explore the caves.

Marsaxlokk: This picturesque fishing village provides a taste of rural Malta with its colorful fishing boats and authentic seafood restaurants.

The Buskett Gardens: A green oasis in the heart of Malta, it's a great place for a nature walk or a picnic.

Majjistral Nature and History Park: Located in the northwest of Malta, this park is a nature lover's paradise with hiking trails and pristine coastline.

Gozo's Countryside: The rural landscapes of Gozo offer opportunities for hiking, biking, and exploring charming villages.

Whether you're a history enthusiast, a beach lover, or someone seeking the serenity of nature, Malta has something to offer for every type of traveler.

Chapter Five

# Dining and Cuisine

## Maltese Food and Specialties

Maltese cuisine is influenced by various Mediterranean cultures and has some unique specialties. Some popular Maltese dishes include:

Pastizzi: These are flaky pastries filled with either ricotta cheese or mushy peas and are a staple snack in Malta.

Rabbit Stew (Fenkata): Rabbit is a popular meat in Maltese cuisine and is often stewed in wine and spices.

Ftira: A traditional Maltese bread that can be filled with various ingredients, similar to a sandwich.

Lampuki Pie: A savory pie made with lampuki fish, vegetables, and herbs.

Bragioli: Beef olives stuffed with bacon, egg, and other ingredients, served with a tomato sauce.

Kapunata: Maltese ratatouille, made with eggplants, tomatoes, and capers.

Kinnie: A popular Maltese soft drink with a unique bitter-sweet taste.

Gbejniet: Small cheeselets made from goat's or sheep's milk, often served with bread and olive oil.

These are just a few examples of Maltese food. The cuisine is known for its rich flavors and the influence of its historical connections to various Mediterranean cultures.

# Restaurants and Local Eateries

Malta, with its rich history and diverse culinary influences, boasts a vibrant dining scene with a wide range of restaurants and local eateries to explore. Whether you're a fan of traditional Maltese cuisine, international dishes, or something in between, you'll find options to satisfy your taste buds.

Traditional Maltese Restaurants: Start by indulging in the authentic flavors of Malta. Many restaurants across the islands offer traditional Maltese dishes, including rabbit stew (fenkata), pastizzi, and fish dishes. Ta' Kris in Valletta is a popular choice, known for its cozy atmosphere and a menu filled with local delicacies.

Seafood Restaurants: Given Malta's location in the Mediterranean, seafood is a prominent part of the cuisine. You can savor freshly caught fish and seafood at places like The Boat House in Marsaxlokk, a fishing village famous for its Sunday fish market.

Italian Cuisine: Malta's historical ties to Italy have left a mark on its culinary landscape. You can find excellent Italian restaurants, such as Tarragon in St. Julian's, serving up delicious pasta, pizzas, and more.

International Fusion: Many restaurants in Malta combine global influences with local ingredients. The Chophouse in Sliema is known for its blend of traditional and contemporary dishes, showcasing the best of local produce.

Cafés and Bakeries: For a quick bite or a sweet treat, visit one of Malta's charming cafés and bakeries. Enjoy Maltese ftira sandwiches or pastries with a cup of coffee. Busy Bee in Gzira is famous for its pastizzi and other savory pastries.

Wine Bars: Malta has a growing wine culture, and you can explore local and international wines at wine bars like Trabuxu Wine Bar in Valletta. They often serve tapas-style dishes to pair with your wine.

Street Food and Food Trucks: Don't miss out on street food options like the Maltese sausage (qassatat) or street vendors selling fresh fruit. Food trucks can be found in popular tourist areas, offering quick and tasty bites.

Rooftop Dining: Enjoy panoramic views while dining at rooftop restaurants, especially in Valletta and St. Julian's. These venues offer a romantic atmosphere for a special evening.

Local Markets: Explore local food markets like the Marsaxlokk Fish Market and the Ta' Qali Farmers' Market to sample fresh produce, cheeses, and other specialties.

Malta's dining scene caters to a variety of preferences and budgets, from casual eateries to upscale fine dining establishments. It's a delightful experience to explore the culinary treasures of this Mediterranean gem and indulge in the unique flavors that Malta has to offer.

# Street Food and Markets

Malta's street food and markets offer a delightful journey into the heart of its culinary culture. These vibrant places allow you to experience the flavors, aromas, and local traditions of the islands. Here's an elaborate look at Malta's street food and markets:

**Street Food:**

Pastizzi: Pastizzi are perhaps the most iconic Maltese street food. These flaky pastries come in two main varieties – one filled with ricotta cheese (pastizz) and the other with a mixture of mushy peas (qassatat). They're widely available and make for a delicious and inexpensive snack.

Maltese Sausage: You'll find stalls and food trucks selling Maltese sausage (zalzett tal-Malti). It's a flavorful pork sausage, often served in ftira bread with mustard and ketchup.

Bread with Toppings: Ftira is a traditional Maltese bread, somewhat similar to pizza dough. It's often sliced open and filled with various toppings like tomato paste, tuna, olives, capers, and more.

Fried Rabbit: Some street food vendors offer fried rabbit, a local delicacy, which can be a bit of a heavier option, but it's a must-try for those seeking an authentic taste of Maltese cuisine.

Fresh Fruit Stalls: You can easily find stalls selling fresh, locally grown fruits, which are perfect for a quick and healthy snack while exploring the streets.

**Markets**:

Marsaxlokk Fish Market: Located in the picturesque fishing village of Marsaxlokk, this market is famous for its colorful fishing boats and the Sunday fish market. It's a seafood lover's paradise, with stalls piled high with freshly caught fish and seafood.

Ta' Qali Farmers' Market: Open on weekdays, Ta' Qali Market offers a wide variety of fresh produce, local cheeses, honey, and traditional Maltese products. It's an excellent place to sample and purchase local specialties.

Valletta Food Market: This historic food market, also known as Is-Suq tal-Belt, is housed in a beautifully restored building in Valletta. It features stalls selling fresh produce, meats, cheeses, and a variety of artisanal products.

Birgu (Vittoriosa) Market: Held on Tuesdays, this market offers a taste of local life. You'll find everything from fresh produce to clothing and household items.

Flea Markets: Malta has various flea markets and bric-a-brac markets where you can hunt for antiques, vintage items, and collectibles, often accompanied by street food vendors.

Craft and Artisan Markets: Some markets, like the Sliema Artisan Market, focus on handmade crafts, jewelry, and artwork. You can often find unique souvenirs and gifts here.

These street food and markets provide a unique opportunity to immerse yourself in Maltese culture, taste authentic dishes, and interact with locals. It's a must-do for food enthusiasts and anyone looking to experience the vibrant and diverse culinary scene of Malta.

# Dietary Preferences

Dietary preferences have become increasingly diverse and personalized, reflecting a growing awareness of the impact of food choices on health, the environment, and ethical considerations. Here's an elaborate look at various dietary preferences:

**Vegetarianism**:

Lacto-Ovo Vegetarian: This is the most common type of vegetarianism, where individuals abstain from meat and fish but include dairy products and eggs in their diet.

Vegan: Vegans avoid all animal products, including meat, dairy, eggs, and often honey. Their diet consists of plant-based foods only.
Pescetarianism: Pescetarians include fish and seafood in their vegetarian diet while avoiding other meats. This choice is often made for health reasons or to reduce the environmental impact of meat consumption.

Flexitarianism: Flexitarians primarily follow a vegetarian diet but occasionally include meat or fish. They focus on plant-based foods but have the flexibility to consume animal products on occasion.

Ketogenic Diet: The ketogenic diet is a high-fat, low-carbohydrate diet that forces the body into a state of ketosis, where it burns fat for energy. It's frequently used to treat specific medical ailments and lose weight.

Paleo Diet: The paleo diet emulates the eating habits of our Paleolithic ancestors, focusing on whole foods such as lean meats, fish, fruits, vegetables, nuts, and seeds while avoiding processed foods, grains, and dairy.

Gluten-Free Diet: Individuals with celiac disease or gluten sensitivity eliminate gluten-containing grains like wheat, barley, and rye. The gluten-free diet has also gained popularity for perceived health benefits.

Mediterranean Diet: Based on the traditional dietary patterns of Mediterranean countries, this diet emphasizes fruits, vegetables, whole grains, olive oil, fish, and moderate consumption of wine. It's linked to both longevity and heart health.

Plant-Based Diet: Plant-based diets are centered on whole, plant foods. While some are vegans or vegetarians, others may include small amounts of animal products. Plant-based diets promote health and environmental sustainability.

Raw Food Diet: Raw foodists consume uncooked and unprocessed foods, such as fruits, vegetables, nuts, and seeds. Advocates believe that this diet retains more nutrients and enzymes.

Halal and Kosher Diets: These dietary preferences adhere to specific religious dietary laws. Halal dietary guidelines are followed by Muslims, while Kosher dietary laws are observed by Jewish individuals.

Allergen-Free Diets: People with food allergies or intolerances may follow diets that exclude specific allergens like peanuts, tree nuts, soy, or dairy to prevent adverse reactions.

Low-Carb Diet: Low-carb diets, such as the Atkins diet, emphasize reducing carbohydrate intake to promote weight loss and control blood sugar levels.

Intermittent Fasting: This eating pattern alternates between periods of eating and fasting. It can take various forms, like the 16/8 method, where one fasts for 16 hours and eats during an 8-hour window.

Alkaline Diet: Advocates of this diet believe that consuming alkaline foods helps maintain the body's pH balance, promoting overall health. It involves eating more fruits, vegetables, and less acidic foods.

Carnivore Diet: On the opposite end of the spectrum, the carnivore diet consists mainly of animal products, with little to no plant-based foods. Proponents argue it provides health benefits, but it's highly controversial.

Fruitarian Diet: Fruitarians primarily eat fruits, nuts, seeds, and other plant parts that can be harvested without harming the plant. It's a highly restrictive diet.

Ayurvedic Diet: Rooted in Ayurvedic medicine, this diet is personalized based on an individual's dosha (body type) and focuses on achieving balance through specific foods and spices.

These dietary preferences reflect the diverse ways in which people choose to nourish their bodies, guided by a range of factors including health, ethics, culture, and personal beliefs. It's important to make dietary choices that align with one's individual needs and values while ensuring they receive the essential nutrients for a balanced diet.

Chapter Six

# Malta's Activities and Entertainment

## Water Sports and Recreation

Malta, surrounded by the stunning Mediterranean Sea, offers a plethora of water sports and recreational activities. From vibrant diving experiences exploring underwater caves and historic shipwrecks to exhilarating windsurfing along the picturesque coastline, Malta caters to both adrenaline enthusiasts and those seeking a more tranquil aquatic experience.

The island's crystal-clear waters provide an ideal setting for snorkeling, allowing visitors to discover the vibrant marine life and colorful coral reefs. Boat trips and sailing excursions are popular, offering a unique perspective of Malta's rugged cliffs and hidden coves.

For a more relaxed day by the sea, Malta's beaches provide sunbathing and swimming opportunities, with golden sands and inviting waters. Additionally, the coastal promenades offer scenic walks, perfect for those who prefer to enjoy the sea breeze at a leisurely pace.

In the evenings, the waterfront comes alive with lively restaurants, bars, and open-air venues, providing a vibrant nightlife scene. Whether you're into savoring local cuisine with a sea view or dancing under the stars, Malta's coastal entertainment ensures a memorable experience for every visitor.

# Hiking and Adventure

Malta, despite its small size, boasts a surprising array of hiking trails and adventurous activities, making it a haven for nature enthusiasts and thrill-seekers alike. The islands' diverse landscapes, ranging from rocky cliffs to lush valleys, provide a scenic backdrop for exploration.

Hiking trails crisscross the countryside, offering a mix of difficulty levels suitable for both beginners and experienced trekkers. The Dingli Cliffs, with their breathtaking views of the Mediterranean, provide a captivating hiking experience, while the picturesque coastal paths around Gozo showcase the island's rugged beauty.

For a more challenging adventure, rock climbing enthusiasts can explore the cliffs of Wied Babu or Wied il-Mielaħ, combining stunning vistas with an adrenaline-pumping ascent. The island's unique geography also allows for exciting activities like abseiling and cliff diving in selected locations.

Exploring Malta's historical sites can be an adventure in itself. The ancient trails around Mdina, the Silent City, take you on a journey through time, unraveling the island's rich history as you traverse medieval streets and fortress walls.

Beyond hiking, Malta offers thrilling water-based activities such as sea kayaking and coasteering, blending exploration with a dash of adrenaline. These adventures reveal hidden sea caves, secluded beaches, and the mesmerizing underwater world.

In essence, Malta's hiking and adventure scene encapsulates the perfect fusion of nature, history, and excitement, ensuring that every step on the islands is a captivating exploration.

# Nightlife and Entertainment

Malta's nightlife is a vibrant tapestry of diverse experiences, offering something for everyone as the sun sets. The island comes alive with an array of entertainment options that cater to various tastes and preferences.

The bustling streets of Paceville in St. Julian's are synonymous with nightlife in Malta. This district is a hub of energy, featuring numerous bars, clubs, and lounges. Whether you're into pulsating beats, live music, or cozy cocktail bars, Paceville has it all. The eclectic mix of venues ensures a dynamic atmosphere, making it a go-to destination for those seeking a lively night out.

Valletta, Malta's capital, offers a more sophisticated and cultural nightlife experience. The city comes alive with events like theater performances, classical concerts, and art exhibitions. Trendy wine bars and waterfront cafes provide a charming setting for a more relaxed evening, where you can enjoy a drink while soaking in the historic ambiance.

Gozo, Malta's sister island, boasts a more laid-back nightlife, with seaside pubs and local festivals. The relaxed atmosphere and scenic surroundings create an ideal setting for a leisurely night with friends or loved ones.

Malta's traditional village festas, held throughout the summer, add a unique touch to the nightlife scene. These celebrations feature lively processions, fireworks, and local bands, creating a festive atmosphere that embodies the spirit of the Maltese culture.

In essence, Malta's nightlife is a kaleidoscope of experiences, from the high-energy beats of Paceville to the cultural richness of Valletta and the charming simplicity of Gozo. Whether you're a party enthusiast or someone looking for a more refined evening, Malta's diverse entertainment options ensure that the night is as captivating as the day.

# Cultural Festivals

Malta's cultural festivals are a vibrant celebration of the island's rich history, traditions, and artistic prowess. Throughout the year, these festivals immerse locals and visitors alike in a kaleidoscope of events, showcasing the diverse facets of Maltese culture.

The most renowned cultural event is undoubtedly the Malta International Arts Festival, an extravaganza that spans various artistic disciplines.

From theater and dance to visual arts and music, this festival transforms Valletta into a hub of creativity, attracting artists and performers from around the globe.

The Malta Jazz Festival is a highlight for music enthusiasts, featuring world-class jazz performances against the backdrop of historic venues like the Grand Harbour. The festival brings together renowned international musicians, creating an unforgettable experience for jazz aficionados.

Għanafest celebrates Malta's traditional folk music, or Għana, with performances by local and international artists. Held in the beautiful Argotti Gardens, this festival provides a unique opportunity to experience the soulful tunes and storytelling that characterize Maltese folk music.

For those fascinated by history, the Medieval Mdina Festival takes visitors on a journey back in time. The ancient streets of Mdina, Malta's former capital, become a stage for reenactments, pageantry, and medieval-themed events, offering a captivating glimpse into the island's past.

Religious festivals, such as the feast of St. Paul's Shipwreck and the Good Friday processions, showcase Malta's deep-rooted religious traditions. These events are marked by elaborate processions, church decorations, and a strong sense of community participation.

In essence, Malta's cultural festivals form a dynamic tapestry that weaves together contemporary and traditional expressions of art, music, and heritage. Attending these events not only provides a deeper understanding of Malta's cultural identity but also offers a memorable and immersive experience for those eager to explore the island's diverse cultural landscape.

Chapter Seven

# Shopping in Malta

## Souvenirs and Local Crafts

In Malta, shopping for souvenirs and local crafts is a vibrant experience that allows you to immerse yourself in the rich cultural tapestry of the islands. From bustling markets to quaint artisan shops, there's an array of treasures waiting to be discovered.

Explore the vibrant street markets, like the Marsaxlokk Fish Market, where you can find an assortment of handmade items reflecting Malta's traditional craftsmanship. Intricately woven lace, known as "bizzilla," is a Maltese specialty, showcasing the skillful artistry passed down through generations.

Visit Mdina Glass to witness the creation of exquisite glassware, from colorful vases to delicate figurines. The Mdina Glass factory not only offers a visual spectacle of glassblowing but also allows you to take home a piece of Malta's contemporary artistry.

For a taste of local flavor, seek out the Ta' Qali Crafts Village, where artisans craft pottery, leather goods, and intricate filigree jewelry. The village provides a charming setting to witness skilled hands transforming raw materials into unique and culturally significant mementos.

Don't forget to pick up a few pieces of Maltese ceramics, adorned with vibrant patterns and designs inspired by the island's history and folklore. These make for both aesthetically pleasing and culturally rich keepsakes.

In summary, shopping for souvenirs and local crafts in Malta is an enchanting journey through the island's artistic heritage, offering a diverse range of handmade treasures that encapsulate the spirit of this Mediterranean gem.

# Popular Shopping Districts

Malta boasts an array of popular shopping districts that cater to diverse tastes, from high-end fashion enthusiasts to those seeking unique local finds. Let's explore some of the prominent shopping areas that add flair to the Maltese retail experience.

1. **Republic Street, Valletta:**
As the main thoroughfare in Malta's capital city, Republic Street in Valletta is a bustling hub of

activity. Lined with a mix of international brands, local boutiques, and quaint cafes, it offers a charming blend of modern and traditional shopping. The historic architecture adds a unique backdrop to your shopping excursion.

### 2. **Sliema Ferries Promenade**:
For those with a penchant for waterfront shopping, Sliema Ferries Promenade is a must-visit. With stunning views of Valletta across the harbor, this area is adorned with designer outlets, trendy boutiques, and artisanal shops. Take a leisurely stroll along the promenade while exploring the diverse retail offerings.

### 3. **The Point Shopping Mall, Sliema**:
The Point is a contemporary shopping mall that caters to fashion-forward individuals. Housing international brands and stylish boutiques, it provides a modern and air-conditioned shopping experience. The mall's selection of restaurants and cafes also makes it a delightful destination for a day of indulgence.

### 4. **Bay Street Shopping Complex, St. Julian's:**
Situated in the heart of St. Julian's, Bay Street Shopping Complex is a vibrant hub for both shopping and entertainment. This open-air mall features a mix of fashion outlets, electronics stores, and eateries. Live performances and events often add an extra layer of excitement to the shopping experience.

5. **Main Street, Mosta:**
For a more local and traditional vibe, Main Street in Mosta is a charming destination. Lined with family-run shops, this area offers a glimpse into everyday Maltese life. Explore the small stores selling handmade crafts, jewelry, and souvenirs while soaking in the laid-back atmosphere.

In essence, Malta's popular shopping districts provide a diverse range of experiences, catering to various preferences and ensuring that retail therapy on the islands is a delightful adventure. Whether you're drawn to historical streets or contemporary malls, Malta has a shopping district to suit your style.

# Markets and Bazaars

Exploring the markets and bazaars of Malta is like embarking on a sensory journey, where vibrant colors, enticing aromas, and the buzz of lively exchanges create an immersive experience. Let's delve into some of the captivating markets that capture the essence of Maltese culture.

1. **Marsaxlokk Fish Market**:
Nestled in the picturesque fishing village of Marsaxlokk, this market is a vibrant tapestry of

sights and sounds. As fishermen unload their fresh catch, the market comes alive with stalls offering an array of seafood, local produce, and handmade crafts. It's a feast for the senses, with the added charm of traditional Luzzu boats bobbing in the harbor.

### 2. **Valletta's Merchants Street Market**:
For a taste of daily life in the capital, head to Merchants Street Market in Valletta. This bustling market is a treasure trove of fresh fruits, vegetables, cheeses, and local specialties. Stroll through the narrow lanes, engage with friendly vendors, and discover the seasonal delights that grace the stalls.

### 3. **Ta' Qali Crafts Village Market:**
Set against the backdrop of the Ta' Qali Crafts Village, this market celebrates Maltese craftsmanship. Artisans showcase their talents through handmade pottery, intricate lacework, and unique souvenirs. It's a fantastic opportunity to witness traditional skills in action and acquire one-of-a-kind pieces directly from the creators.

### 4. **Birgu Market:**
Step into the historic town of Birgu and experience its charming market, where locals and visitors alike converge to explore an eclectic mix of stalls. From fresh produce to handmade jewelry, the market reflects the community's vibrant spirit. The medieval

surroundings add a touch of history to this lively gathering.

5. **Victoria Market, Gozo**:
Venture to Gozo, Malta's sister island, to discover the bustling Victoria Market. This market offers an authentic Gozitan experience, with stalls brimming with local cheeses, handmade crafts, and traditional snacks. The friendly atmosphere and genuine hospitality make it a must-visit for those seeking a taste of Gozo's unique charm.

In summary, Malta's markets and bazaars provide an enchanting panorama of the island's diverse offerings. From the daily hustle of Valletta's markets to the cultural richness of crafts villages, each market is a microcosm of Maltese life, inviting you to immerse yourself in the local tapestry.

# Duty-Free Shopping

Duty-free shopping in Malta adds an extra layer of allure to the retail experience, allowing travelers to indulge in premium goods at advantageous prices. Here's an exploration of the duty-free offerings in Malta:

1. **Malta International Airport:**
As the primary gateway to the islands, Malta International Airport boasts a sophisticated

duty-free shopping area. From high-end fashion brands to luxury watches and cosmetics, the selection caters to a diverse range of preferences. The electronics section is particularly noteworthy, offering the latest gadgets and tech accessories at competitive prices.

### 2. Sea and Air Terminal, Valletta:
For those arriving by cruise ship, the Sea and Air Terminal in Valletta provides a duty-free shopping haven. The waterfront location enhances the experience, offering panoramic views of the Grand Harbor while you peruse an array of tax-free goods. This terminal is a convenient stop for travelers eager to make the most of duty-free opportunities.

### 3. Ferry Terminals to Gozo:
Even the ferry terminals connecting Malta to Gozo feature duty-free shopping, allowing passengers to shop for a variety of products while enjoying a scenic journey. From spirits and tobacco to perfumes and souvenirs, these terminals offer a chance to grab tax-free bargains before exploring the sister island.

### 4. Specialized Duty-Free Stores:
Beyond transportation hubs, specialized duty-free stores in popular tourist areas such as Sliema and St. Julian's cater to the discerning shopper. These stores often focus on luxury items, including designer fashion, accessories, and premium spirits.

The allure of tax-free pricing enhances the appeal of indulging in high-quality goods.

### 5. **Exclusive Duty-Free Events:**

Malta occasionally hosts exclusive duty-free events, enticing shoppers with limited-time offers and promotions. These events often feature collaborations with renowned brands, adding an element of exclusivity to the shopping experience. Keep an eye on local event calendars to catch these special opportunities.

In essence, duty-free shopping in Malta goes beyond mere transactions; it becomes a part of the travel experience, allowing visitors to acquire premium goods at more favorable prices. The strategic locations of duty-free outlets, combined with a diverse range of products, make it a tempting proposition for those looking to indulge in a bit of retail therapy while exploring the Maltese islands.

Chapter Eight

# **Practical Information**

## Health and Safety

Malta is a beautiful Mediterranean archipelago that is known for its rich history, stunning landscapes, and vibrant culture. When it comes to health and safety, Malta is generally a safe destination for travelers. However, it's important to be aware of certain practical information to ensure a safe and enjoyable visit. Here's an overview of health and safety considerations in Malta:

**Medical Facilities:**

Malta has a well-developed healthcare system with modern hospitals and medical facilities. The main public hospital is the Mater Dei Hospital in Msida, while there are also private hospitals and clinics. Pharmacies are widespread and easy to find, and many common medications are available over the counter.
Health Insurance:

It's highly recommended for travelers to have comprehensive travel insurance that covers medical expenses. If you are an EU citizen, you

92

can use your European Health Insurance Card (EHIC) for necessary medical treatment.

Emergency Services:

The emergency number in Malta is 112, which you can call for police, fire, or medical emergencies.

Water Quality:

In Malta, the tap water is safe to consume. It meets European Union standards for quality and is readily available.

Vaccinations:

There are no specific vaccinations required for travelers to Malta. Staying up to date on routine vaccines is usually a smart idea.

**Safety**:

Malta is considered a safe destination for tourists. Violent crime is rare, but like in any place, you should still take common-sense precautions, such as safeguarding your belongings.

Traffic and Driving:

Maltese roads can be narrow and winding, and traffic can be congested, especially in urban areas. Be cautious when driving and make sure to have the necessary documentation, including an international driver's permit if required.

Sun Protection:

Malta enjoys a Mediterranean climate, and the sun can be quite intense. It's crucial to use sunscreen, wear a hat, and stay hydrated, especially during the hot summer months.

Food Safety:

Maltese cuisine is delicious, but it's important to be cautious about food safety. If your stomach is sensitive, stay away from street food and only eat at respectable establishments.

Emergency Evacuation:

Familiarize yourself with the location of your country's embassy or consulate in Malta. They are capable of helping in an emergency.

Natural Hazards:

While Malta doesn't face significant natural disasters, it's a good idea to be aware of potential risks. For example, in the rare event of severe weather conditions, stay informed through local authorities.

COVID-19 Considerations:

Due to the ongoing COVID-19 pandemic, there might be specific health and safety measures in place, such as mask mandates, social distancing, or vaccination requirements. Stay updated on the latest travel advisories and local regulations. Remember that while Malta is generally a safe and welcoming destination, taking the necessary precautions and staying informed will help ensure a trouble-free and enjoyable visit. Always check the latest travel advisories from your government and the Maltese authorities before your trip to stay updated on any specific health and safety guidelines.

# Local Customs and Etiquette

Malta, a Mediterranean archipelago, has a rich cultural heritage reflected in its local customs and etiquette. Here's an overview:

Greetings and Politeness:

Maltese people are generally warm and friendly. A handshake is a common greeting.
Titles are important, and it's customary to use titles such as "Mr." or "Mrs." until invited to use first names.

Language:

While English is widely spoken, the official languages are Maltese and English. Learning a few Maltese phrases is appreciated.

Dress Code:

Dressing modestly is respected, especially in religious sites. Swimwear should be confined to beaches and pools.

Religious Sensitivity:

Malta is predominantly Roman Catholic. It's customary to dress conservatively when visiting churches, and visitors should show respect during religious events and ceremonies.

Social Customs:

Family is highly valued, and social gatherings often revolve around family events. It's common to greet with a kiss on both cheeks among close acquaintances.
Being punctual is appreciated, although a slight delay may be tolerated in a social context.

Dining Etiquette:

Bringing a little gift is usual when one is invited to someone's home. Dining is a social event, and meals are often enjoyed leisurely.
It's polite to taste a bit of everything and express appreciation for the meal.

Festivals and Celebrations:

Malta celebrates numerous festivals, many with religious significance. The most famous is Carnival, marked by colorful parades and events.
During festivals, expect lively street celebrations, processions, and traditional music.

Superstitions:

Maltese culture has its share of superstitions. For instance, the Evil Eye is believed to bring bad luck, so you may see charms to ward it off.

Traffic and Driving:

The left side of the road is where drivers drive. Pedestrians should be cautious when crossing, as traffic can be busy.

Environmental Respect:

Malta treasures its natural beauty, so it's essential to be mindful of the environment. Littering is

frowned upon, and care should be taken when exploring historical or natural sites.
Understanding and respecting these customs contribute to a positive experience in Malta, fostering connections with the locals and immersing oneself in the unique cultural tapestry of the islands.

Hospitality:

Maltese hospitality is renowned. If invited into a Maltese home, it's customary to express gratitude for the invitation and for the hospitality received. Complimenting the host's home is also appreciated.
Manners in Public Places:

Queuing is common in Malta, and it's expected to wait your turn patiently. Being polite in public spaces, such as buses or shops, is valued.

Marketplace Etiquette:

Haggling is not a common practice in Maltese markets. Prices are generally fixed, and attempting to negotiate too aggressively may be seen as disrespectful.

Respect for Elders:

Respect for elders is deeply ingrained in Maltese culture. It's customary to show deference and courtesy towards older individuals.

Expressions of Affection:

Maltese people are expressive and affectionate. It's not uncommon to see friends or family members hugging and kissing in public.

Water Conservation:

Due to its semi-arid climate, water conservation is crucial in Malta. Visitors are encouraged to use water responsibly and be mindful of its scarcity.

Tipping Etiquette:

Tipping is customary in restaurants, and a service charge may be included. It's nice to leave a little gratuity for excellent service.

Art and Craft Appreciation:

Malta has a rich tradition of arts and crafts. Supporting local artisans and appreciating traditional crafts, such as filigree jewelry and handmade lace, is a positive gesture.

Cultural Sensitivity:

Malta has a diverse cultural history influenced by various civilizations. Being sensitive to this diversity and avoiding stereotypes fosters understanding and appreciation.

Island Time:

The pace of life in Malta is generally relaxed. Embracing the unhurried atmosphere and adapting to the local concept of time enhances the overall experience.
By immersing yourself in these nuanced aspects of Maltese customs, you'll not only navigate social situations more smoothly but also gain a deeper appreciation for the rich cultural fabric of this Mediterranean archipelago.

# Emergency Contacts

Having access to emergency contacts is crucial when you're traveling, especially in an unfamiliar destination like Malta. Here's a list of essential emergency contacts to keep handy during your stay:

**Police Emergency**: For immediate police assistance, dial 112. This number connects you to the police, fire services, and ambulance services.

**Ambulance and Medical Emergency Services:** In the event of a medical emergency, dial 112 to request an ambulance. The operator will dispatch the necessary medical assistance to your location.

**Fire and Rescue Services**: If you encounter a fire or require assistance in a rescue situation, dial 112 to contact the fire and rescue services.

**Tourist Helpline**: The Malta Tourism Authority operates a tourist helpline, providing assistance and information to tourists. You can reach them at +356 21692447 or via email at info@visitmalta.com.

**Embassy or Consulate Contact**: If you are a foreign national, it's vital to have the contact information of your country's embassy or consulate in Malta. They can provide assistance in case of legal issues, lost passports, or other emergencies. Make sure you have easy access to their contact details.

**Local Hospital and Medical Facilities**: Keep the contact information of local hospitals and medical facilities, such as the Mater Dei Hospital in Msida, along with private clinics and pharmacies. This will come in handy in case of non-emergency medical needs or inquiries.

**Roadside Assistance**: If you're driving in Malta and encounter any vehicle-related issues or breakdowns, having the contact information for a reliable roadside assistance service can be beneficial. Consider researching local automobile associations or private towing services in advance.

**Lost or Stolen Credit Cards**: In the unfortunate event of a lost or stolen credit card, it's important to have the contact information for your bank or credit card issuer. This will enable you to report the incident immediately and prevent any unauthorized transactions.

**Poison Control Center**: While it's not something anyone wishes to use, having the contact information for a poison control center can be crucial in the case of accidental poisoning. Keep the contact details of relevant poison control facilities in Malta readily accessible.

**Consular Services for Foreign Nationals:** Apart from your embassy or consulate, consider noting down the contact information for any international organizations or services that offer support to foreign nationals in Malta. These organizations can provide guidance and assistance in various situations.

By ensuring you have these emergency contacts readily available, you can better prepare yourself for any unexpected situations that may arise during your time in Malta. It's advisable to save these numbers in your phone, have them written down in a secure location, and share them with your travel companions for added safety and convenience.

# Internet and Connectivity

Internet and connectivity in Malta are well-developed, offering tourists and residents convenient access to various communication services. Here's an overview of internet and

**connectivity options in Malta:**

Internet Access: Malta has a robust internet infrastructure, with widespread access to high-speed internet in most urban and rural areas. Many hotels, restaurants, cafes, and public spaces offer free Wi-Fi, making it convenient for tourists to stay connected while exploring the country.

Mobile Networks and SIM Cards: Malta has several reliable mobile network operators, including GO, Vodafone, and Melita. These providers offer a range of prepaid and postpaid SIM card options, allowing visitors to easily access mobile data services during their stay. SIM cards are available for purchase at various outlets, including airports, convenience stores, and telecom shops.

Roaming Services: If you prefer to use your existing mobile phone plan from your home country, check with your mobile service provider about international roaming options and associated costs. It's essential to be aware of potential roaming charges to avoid unexpected expenses.

Public Wi-Fi Hotspots: In addition to hotels and cafes, Malta offers public Wi-Fi hotspots in various locations, including popular tourist attractions, public squares, and transportation hubs. While using public Wi-Fi, it's advisable to employ a virtual private network (VPN) for added security.

Internet Cafes: Although less common than in previous years, internet cafes still exist in Malta, particularly in urban areas and tourist-centric locations. These cafes provide access to computers and internet services for those who may not have their own devices.

Broadband and Fiber Optic Connections: Many households in Malta have access to high-speed broadband and fiber optic internet connections. This reliable infrastructure supports a smooth online experience for both residents and visitors who require consistent and fast internet access for work or leisure activities.

Cybersecurity and Data Privacy: While using the internet in Malta, it's essential to prioritize cybersecurity and protect your personal data. Ensure that your devices have updated security software and avoid connecting to unsecured or public networks when handling sensitive information.

Internet Service Providers (ISPs): Major ISPs in Malta, such as GO and Melita, offer a variety of internet packages tailored to different user requirements. These providers offer a range of plans, including home broadband, mobile internet, and bundled services that include TV and phone packages.

Online Services and Apps: Many popular online services and apps are available in Malta, including food delivery platforms, ride-hailing services, and online shopping platforms. These services leverage the robust internet infrastructure, providing convenience and accessibility to both locals and visitors.

By taking advantage of Malta's advanced internet and connectivity services, visitors can stay connected, access essential information, and make the most of their time in the country. Whether for leisure, work, or staying in touch with loved ones, Malta's reliable internet infrastructure ensures a seamless online experience for all.

Chapter Nine

# Travel Tips and Resources

## Packing Tips

When preparing for a trip to Malta, it's essential to pack smartly, considering the Mediterranean climate and the specific activities you plan to engage in. Here are some detailed packing tips to ensure you have a comfortable and enjoyable experience:

Clothing: Malta's climate is typically warm and sunny, especially during the summer months, so pack lightweight, breathable clothing such as cotton shirts, shorts, and sundresses. Don't forget to bring comfortable walking shoes for exploring the historic sites and rugged terrain. If you plan to visit during the cooler months, include a light jacket or sweater for the evenings, as temperatures can drop.

Swimwear and Beach Essentials: Given Malta's stunning coastline and clear blue waters, it's wise to pack swimwear, beach towels, and protective gear like hats, sunglasses, and sunscreen. Including a rash guard or a light cover-up can be helpful, especially for those with sensitive skin.

Sightseeing Necessities: As Malta is rich in historical and cultural landmarks, it's advisable to carry a reliable camera, along with extra batteries and memory cards, to capture the breathtaking sights. Additionally, bring a small backpack to carry water, snacks, and any essentials during your explorations.

Electronics and Adapters: Remember to pack the necessary electrical adapters and converters, as Malta uses the British three-pin rectangular plug. If you plan to use electronic devices such as laptops or smartphones, ensure you have the appropriate adapters to keep them charged throughout your trip.

Travel Documents: Don't forget to carry your passport, travel insurance documents, and any other necessary identification. It's also beneficial to have copies of these documents stored separately in case of loss or theft.

Medication and Toiletries: Bring any prescription medication you may need during your stay. Additionally, pack a basic first-aid kit with essentials such as pain relievers, antihistamines, and any personal medications. Remember to include toiletries like sunscreen, insect repellent, and basic skincare products to protect yourself from the sun and keep your skin healthy.

Travel Accessories: Consider packing a reusable water bottle to stay hydrated, a travel guide or map for easy navigation, and a money belt or a secure bag to keep your valuables safe while you explore the island.

By considering these detailed packing tips, you can ensure a smooth and comfortable journey to Malta, allowing you to fully immerse yourself in the beauty and culture of this vibrant Mediterranean destination.

# Money-Saving Strategies

When planning a trip to Malta, implementing effective money-saving strategies can help you make the most of your budget without compromising on your travel experience. The following are some thorough tactics to think about:

Travel Off-Season: Opting to visit Malta during the shoulder seasons, such as spring or fall, can lead to significant cost savings on accommodation and flights. Not only are prices generally lower during these periods, but you'll also have the advantage of enjoying a less crowded experience, allowing you to explore popular attractions without the usual tourist rush.

Accommodation Options: Explore a variety of accommodation options, including budget-friendly hotels, hostels, guesthouses, or vacation rentals. You can get the best bargains by making reservations in advance and researching costs across several websites. Additionally, consider staying slightly outside popular tourist areas to find more affordable lodging options while still having convenient access to attractions.

Local Dining Experience: To save on food expenses, try dining where the locals eat. Explore traditional Maltese eateries and markets that offer authentic, affordable cuisine. Consider sampling local street food and regional specialties, which can be both delicious and cost-effective compared to dining in upscale restaurants aimed at tourists.

Public Transportation and Walking: Utilize Malta's efficient public transportation system, including buses and ferries, to get around the island. Opting for multi-day or weekly travel passes can often result in substantial savings compared to individual ticket purchases. Additionally, take advantage of Malta's walkable cities and towns, which can help you save on transportation costs while allowing you to immerse yourself in the local culture and scenery.

Discounts and Free Attractions: Research any available discounts, such as student or senior discounts, for attractions, tours, and activities. Take advantage of free or low-cost attractions, including public parks, beaches, and historic sites, which can provide enriching experiences without straining your budget.

Water and Snacks: Purchase water from local supermarkets or convenience stores instead of buying it from tourist areas, where prices are typically inflated. Similarly, bring your own snacks or pack a picnic for days when you'll be exploring for extended periods, as this can help you avoid unnecessary expenses at tourist-centric cafes and eateries.

Souvenir Shopping: Exercise caution when purchasing souvenirs and gifts, as tourist-heavy areas often charge higher prices. Consider exploring local markets and independent shops for unique and reasonably priced souvenirs that reflect Malta's rich culture and heritage.

By incorporating these detailed money-saving strategies into your travel plans, you can enjoy an enriching and budget-friendly experience in Malta, making the most of your time on the stunning Mediterranean island without overspending.

# Travel Apps and Websites

When planning a trip to Malta, utilizing various travel apps and websites can significantly enhance your travel experience, making it more convenient and enjoyable. Here are some useful travel apps and websites that can assist you in different aspects of your journey:

1. Google Maps: Google Maps is a versatile navigation app that can help you explore Malta's streets and landmarks, find nearby attractions, restaurants, and public transportation options, and plan efficient routes for your daily activities.

2. TripAdvisor: TripAdvisor provides a comprehensive platform for researching and booking accommodations, restaurants, and attractions. It offers valuable insights from traveler reviews and ratings, helping you make informed decisions about where to stay, dine, and visit during your trip.

3. Airbnb: Airbnb is a popular platform that offers a wide range of accommodation options, including apartments, houses, and unique stays. It provides the opportunity to book local accommodations that can offer a more personalized and immersive experience compared to traditional hotels.

4. Skyscanner or Kayak: These flight comparison websites help you find the best deals on flights to

and from Malta, allowing you to compare prices across different airlines and travel dates. They also offer tools to set price alerts and track fluctuations in airfare, enabling you to secure the most cost-effective options.

5. Rome2rio: Rome2rio is a helpful website and app that assists in planning your travel itinerary by providing information on various transportation options, including flights, trains, buses, and ferries. It offers estimated travel times, costs, and routes, allowing you to make informed decisions about your transportation choices.

6. XE Currency or Currency Converter Plus: These currency converter apps help you stay informed about the latest exchange rates, making it easier to manage your expenses and budget effectively during your trip to Malta.

7. Culture Trip or Lonely Planet Guides: These apps offer valuable insights into Malta's culture, history, and local attractions, providing comprehensive travel guides, recommendations, and tips for exploring the island's hidden gems and must-visit destinations.

By utilizing these travel apps and websites, you can streamline your travel planning process, access valuable information, and make informed decisions to ensure a seamless and enriching experience during your visit to Malta.

Chapter Ten

# Sample Itineraries

## 3-Day Highlights of Malta

Here's a comprehensive 3-day itinerary highlighting the best of Malta:

**Day 1:** Exploring Valletta and Mdina

Morning:
Start your day with a visit to St. John's Co-Cathedral in Valletta, marveling at its stunning Baroque architecture and Caravaggio's masterpiece, "The Beheading of Saint John the Baptist."
Explore the Upper Barrakka Gardens, enjoying panoramic views of the Grand Harbor and the Three Cities.
Afternoon:
Have a traditional Maltese lunch at a local restaurant, savoring local specialties such as rabbit stew and pastizzi.

Visit the Grand Master's Palace, which houses the Office of the President of Malta and the Armory, displaying an impressive collection of weapons and armor.

Evening:

Take a short drive to Mdina, the Silent City, and wander through its narrow, winding streets, experiencing the medieval charm of this ancient capital.

Enjoy a delightful dinner at one of Mdina's atmospheric restaurants, savoring the local cuisine and the enchanting ambiance.

**Day 2:** Discovering the Maltese Archipelago

Morning:

Embark on a day trip to the Blue Grotto in the southern part of the island, where you can marvel at the stunning natural rock formations and vibrant blue waters.

Afternoon:

Enjoy a leisurely lunch at one of the seaside restaurants in the fishing village of Marsaxlokk, famous for its colorful traditional boats and fresh seafood.

Explore the Hagar Qim and Mnajdra Temples, two UNESCO World Heritage Sites dating back to 3600-3200 BC, and delve into Malta's prehistoric past.

Evening:

Head back to Valletta and spend your evening strolling along the bustling waterfront, enjoying the views and the vibrant atmosphere.

**Day 3**: Coastal Beauty and Cultural Immersion

Morning:
Visit the ancient city of Vittoriosa, one of the Three Cities, and explore its historical sites, such as the Fort St. Angelo and the Inquisitor's Palace.
Afternoon:
Discover the charming town of Sliema, known for its vibrant promenade, bustling shops, and cafes. Enjoy a relaxing lunch with beautiful views of the Mediterranean.
Take a boat tour to the picturesque island of Comino, and swim in the crystal-clear waters of the Blue Lagoon, surrounded by breathtaking natural beauty.
Evening:
End your day with a farewell dinner at a seaside restaurant, enjoying delicious Maltese cuisine and reflecting on the beauty and history you've experienced during your stay in Malta.
This itinerary should provide you with a well-rounded experience, allowing you to immerse yourself in Malta's rich history, stunning architecture, and breathtaking natural beauty. Enjoy your trip!

# Family-Friendly Trip

Here's a detailed 4-day family-friendly itinerary for a memorable trip in Malta:

**Day 1**: Arrival and Beach Fun

Morning:
Arrive in Malta and settle into your family-friendly accommodation.
Head to Mellieha Bay, one of the island's most family-friendly beaches, and spend the morning building sandcastles and enjoying the crystal-clear waters.
Afternoon:
Have a relaxed lunch at one of the beachside restaurants, savoring some delicious Maltese snacks and refreshing drinks.
Explore the nearby Popeye Village, a fun-filled theme park based on the iconic Popeye movie, offering various entertaining activities for children and adults alike.
Evening:
Enjoy a peaceful evening stroll along the beach, taking in the sunset and the calming atmosphere.

**Day 2**: Exploring Fun-filled Attractions

Morning:
Visit the Malta National Aquarium, where your family can discover a variety of marine life and participate in interactive educational activities.

Afternoon:
Have a delightful family lunch at a nearby family-friendly restaurant, offering a variety of cuisines suitable for all ages.
Spend the afternoon at the Esplora Interactive Science Centre, engaging in hands-on exhibits and workshops that will entertain and educate both children and adults.
Evening:
Enjoy a cozy family dinner at your chosen restaurant, discussing the exciting experiences of the day and planning the adventures for the next day.

**Day 3:** Cultural Exploration and Adventure

Morning:
Visit the Malta Toy Museum, a delightful place where your family can explore a vast collection of toys and games from different eras, providing a fun and educational experience for all.
Afternoon:
Enjoy a family-friendly lunch at a traditional Maltese restaurant, introducing your family to the local flavors and specialties.
Explore the Malta Maritime Museum, where you can discover the island's rich maritime history through interactive displays and engaging exhibits suitable for all ages.
Evening:

Take a leisurely stroll through the local markets, indulging in some shopping and trying out local snacks and sweets.

**Day 4:** Nature and Adventure

Morning:
Visit the Splash and Fun Water Park, where your family can enjoy thrilling water rides, slides, and various attractions for a day full of excitement and laughter.
Afternoon:
Have a picnic lunch at one of the nearby parks or gardens, enjoying the serene surroundings and bonding with your family.
Explore the Buskett Gardens and Verdala Palace, taking a nature walk and admiring the lush greenery and beautiful landscapes.
Evening:
Enjoy a cozy family dinner at a local restaurant, reminiscing about the wonderful memories created during your family-friendly trip to Malta.
This itinerary is designed to provide your family with a perfect balance of fun, education, relaxation, and adventure, ensuring an unforgettable and enjoyable experience for everyone. Enjoy your trip!

# Off the Beaten Path Adventures

Here's a detailed 5-day itinerary for those seeking off the beaten path adventures in Malta:

**Day 1:** Coastal Exploration and Hidden Coves

Morning:
Begin your adventure with a visit to Wied il-Ghasri, a secluded and picturesque narrow gorge located on the western coast of Gozo, offering stunning views and a tranquil atmosphere.
Afternoon:
Enjoy a picnic lunch at a quiet spot near the cliffs, savoring the natural beauty and serenity of the surroundings.
Explore the Xwejni Salt Pans, a unique site where you can observe the traditional salt-harvesting process and enjoy the scenic views of the rugged coastline.
Evening:
Experience a sunset hike along the Ta' Cenc Cliffs, immersing yourself in the breathtaking panoramic views and the peaceful ambiance of the unspoiled natural landscape.

**Day 2:** Historical Mysteries and Natural Wonders

Morning:

Venture to the underground world of the Ghar Dalam Cave and Museum, where you can explore a prehistoric cave and learn about Malta's ancient geological history.

Afternoon:

Enjoy a local farm-to-table lunch at a hidden countryside restaurant, savoring fresh and organic Maltese cuisine in a serene and rustic setting.

Discover the mystical Dingli Cliffs, the highest point on the island, and enjoy a peaceful hike, marveling at the stunning vistas of the Mediterranean Sea and the rugged coastline.

Evening:

Dine at a local restaurant known for its traditional Maltese dishes, and immerse yourself in the authentic flavors and warm hospitality of the region.

**Day 3:** Rural Villages and Authentic Experiences

Morning:

Explore the charming village of Gharb in Gozo, known for its traditional architecture, quaint streets, and friendly locals, providing an authentic glimpse into rural Maltese life.

Afternoon:

Indulge in a hearty and traditional Gozitan lunch at a family-run eatery, sampling local delicacies and specialties unique to the region.

Visit the Ta' Pinu Basilica, a sacred pilgrimage site renowned for its religious significance and stunning architecture, offering a serene and contemplative atmosphere.

Evening:
Enjoy a relaxing evening at your chosen accommodation, reflecting on the day's adventures and savoring the tranquility of the rural surroundings.

**Day 4:** Hidden Gems and Secluded Beauty

Morning:
Embark on a trek to the hidden gem of the Fungus Rock, an impressive natural limestone rock formation, and learn about the intriguing folklore associated with it.
Afternoon:
Delight in a picnic lunch at a secluded beach or a quiet countryside spot, relishing the solitude and the unspoiled natural beauty of Malta.
Explore the lesser-known San Blas Bay, a remote and stunning beach known for its reddish sand and clear turquoise waters, perfect for a refreshing swim or a leisurely sunbathing session.
Evening:
Enjoy a quiet dinner at a local restaurant, sharing stories and experiences from your day of exploration and relaxation.

**Day 5:** Cultural Immersion and Farewell

Morning:
Visit the quaint village of Marsaxlokk, renowned for its traditional fishing boats, colorful markets, and

authentic Maltese charm, providing a perfect last-day cultural experience.
Afternoon:
Savor a farewell lunch at a seaside restaurant, indulging in freshly caught seafood and other local delicacies, while taking in the picturesque views of the fishing village.
Evening:
Spend your final moments in Malta reflecting on your unique off the beaten path adventures, cherishing the memories created during your exploration of the island's hidden treasures and lesser-known wonders.

# Romantic Getaway

Here's a detailed 4-day itinerary for a romantic getaway in Malta:

**Day 1**: Arrival and Romantic Evening

Morning:
Arrive in Malta and check into your luxurious accommodation, ideally a charming boutique hotel or a secluded villa with stunning views.
Afternoon:
Enjoy a leisurely lunch at a cozy restaurant with a romantic ambiance, savoring the delectable Mediterranean cuisine and fine local wines.

Take a stroll through the beautiful San Anton Gardens, known for their tranquil atmosphere and picturesque landscapes, perfect for a romantic afternoon walk.

Evening:

Indulge in an intimate candlelit dinner at a renowned fine dining restaurant, relishing the exquisite flavors of gourmet Maltese dishes and enjoying the enchanting atmosphere.

**Day 2:** Island Excursion and Sunset Views

Morning:

Embark on a private boat tour around the islands, exploring hidden coves and secluded beaches, and enjoying the stunning coastal views and the refreshing sea breeze.

Afternoon:

Have a private gourmet picnic on a secluded beach, enjoying each other's company amidst the serene and picturesque surroundings.

Visit the charming town of Rabat, exploring its quaint streets, historical sites, and local shops, creating a romantic and immersive cultural experience.

Evening:

Watch the sunset from the Dingli Cliffs, the highest point on the island, and revel in the breathtaking panoramic views, creating a magical and memorable moment for you and your partner.

**Day 3:** Relaxation and Pampering

Morning:
Enjoy a leisurely breakfast in bed or at a local cafe, savoring a variety of freshly prepared delicacies and enjoying a slow and romantic start to the day.
Afternoon:
Indulge in a couple's spa treatment at a luxurious spa, enjoying massages, wellness treatments, and a tranquil atmosphere conducive to relaxation and rejuvenation.
Have a private lunch at the spa's restaurant, enjoying healthy and nourishing dishes designed to complement your spa experience and promote a sense of well-being.
Evening:
Spend a quiet and intimate evening together, perhaps with a private in-room dinner service, creating an atmosphere of coziness and intimacy.

**Day 4:** Farewell with Unforgettable Memories

Morning:
Enjoy a romantic breakfast with a view, either at your accommodation or at a scenic cafe, cherishing the last moments of your getaway and reminiscing about the beautiful experiences shared.
Afternoon:
Take a leisurely stroll through the charming streets of Valletta, exploring the city's historical landmarks, quaint cafes, and local shops, and perhaps picking

up some souvenirs to remember your romantic escape.
Have a farewell lunch at a charming restaurant with a view, enjoying the delicious food and the beautiful surroundings one last time before departing.
Evening:
Depart from Malta with cherished memories of your romantic getaway, leaving with the promise of returning for more unforgettable moments in the future.

Chapter Eleven

# Beyond Malta

## Day Trips to Gozo and Comino

Malta, a small archipelago in the Mediterranean, offers not only its own rich history and culture but also the opportunity to explore two neighboring islands, Gozo and Comino, on an unforgettable day trip. Let's embark on an immersive journey to these captivating destinations.

Gozo, often referred to as the 'Isle of Calypso' from Homer's epic Odyssey, is renowned for its serene landscapes, rustic charm, and historical significance. A short ferry ride from Malta takes you to this idyllic paradise. Upon arrival, you'll be greeted by panoramic views of rolling hills, quaint villages, and a dramatic coastline that beckons the adventurous spirit.

One of the island's prime attractions is the Citadel, a fortified city dating back to the Bronze Age, offering a glimpse into Gozo's historical past. As you stroll through its winding alleys, you'll discover ancient churches, museums, and captivating architecture that reveal the island's vibrant heritage. The Azure Window, a natural limestone arch jutting out from the sea, once a star of the island, sadly collapsed in 2017, but its remnants still hold a poignant allure.

Delve into Gozo's natural beauty by exploring the Inland Sea and Dwejra Bay, where you can witness breathtaking sunsets and explore the mystical sea caves. The island's unspoiled countryside, dotted with charming farms and vineyards, invites you to savor local produce and immerse yourself in Gozitan culture.

Comino, the smallest of the three islands, is a tranquil haven known for its crystal-clear Blue Lagoon. This natural pool of azure waters is a paradise for swimmers, snorkelers, and divers seeking an enchanting underwater world teeming with marine life. The striking contrast of the lagoon's vivid blue against the rugged coastline makes for a picturesque setting, perfect for capturing memorable moments.

While Comino's size restricts extensive exploration, its unspoiled beauty and tranquil ambiance create an ideal escape from the bustling crowds. Visitors can enjoy leisurely walks along the rugged coastal paths, taking in the island's untouched natural beauty.

For travelers seeking an escape from the hustle and bustle of urban life, these day trips to Gozo and Comino offer a refreshing and invigorating experience, filled with historical discoveries, natural wonders, and the warm hospitality of the Maltese people. Whether you are a history enthusiast, a nature lover, or simply seeking relaxation, these neighboring islands promise a memorable and enriching adventure.

## Exploring Nearby Destinations

Exploring nearby destinations from your current location can lead to remarkable discoveries and enriching experiences. Whether you're seeking a weekend getaway or a day trip, venturing beyond your immediate surroundings can offer a fresh perspective and a chance to immerse yourself in new cultures and landscapes. Here's a detailed guide to help you make the most of your nearby exploration:

Research and Planning: Start by researching nearby destinations that pique your interest. Look into their historical significance, cultural attractions, natural landscapes, and local cuisine. Plan your itinerary, considering travel time, accommodation options, and points of interest to ensure a smooth and enjoyable journey.

Local Culture and Heritage: Embrace the local culture by visiting museums, art galleries, and historical sites that showcase the area's rich heritage. Engage with locals, try regional delicacies, and participate in cultural events to gain a deeper understanding of the community's traditions and way of life.

Natural Wonders and Outdoor Adventures: Explore nearby national parks, hiking trails, or scenic spots that offer breathtaking views and opportunities for outdoor activities. Whether it's a picturesque mountain range, a tranquil lake, or a pristine beach, immersing yourself in nature can rejuvenate your senses and provide a much-needed escape from the daily routine.

Hidden Gems and Off-the-Beaten-Path Attractions: Seek out lesser-known attractions or off-the-beaten-path destinations that may not be as popular but offer unique experiences and a glimpse into the local lifestyle. These hidden gems often reveal the authentic charm and character of a place, allowing you to create lasting memories away from the tourist crowds.

Culinary Delights and Local Cuisine: Indulge in the local cuisine by visiting traditional eateries, street markets, or food festivals that showcase the region's flavors and culinary traditions. Try regional specialties, savor freshly prepared dishes, and learn about the culinary heritage that defines the area's gastronomic identity.

Community Engagement and Social Activities: Consider participating in community-driven initiatives, volunteering opportunities, or local gatherings that foster connections and promote social engagement. Contributing to local projects or getting involved in community events can provide a sense of fulfillment and a deeper connection to the people and places you visit.

Reflection and Relaxation: Take time to relax and reflect on your journey. Whether it's finding a serene spot in nature, enjoying a leisurely stroll through a charming town, or unwinding at a local spa, allow yourself moments of tranquility to appreciate the beauty and serenity of your surroundings.

By embracing the essence of nearby exploration, you can uncover the hidden treasures and unique experiences that lie just a stone's throw away, fostering a deeper appreciation for the diversity and beauty of the world around you.

Chapter Twelve

# Traveling Responsibly

## Environmental Initiatives

Malta, a picturesque island nation in the Mediterranean, has been taking significant strides in promoting responsible and sustainable tourism. Recognizing the importance of preserving its natural beauty and cultural heritage, Malta has implemented various environmental initiatives to mitigate the negative impacts of tourism on its delicate ecosystem.

One of the key measures undertaken by Malta is the promotion of eco-friendly practices within the tourism industry. Several hotels and resorts have adopted sustainable practices, including energy-efficient operations, waste reduction, and water conservation. Additionally, the local authorities have encouraged the use of renewable energy sources and the implementation of eco-friendly transportation options to reduce the carbon footprint.

Furthermore, the Maltese government has invested in the preservation and restoration of its historical and natural sites, aiming to maintain their integrity while allowing visitors to appreciate the rich history and biodiversity of the island. Through initiatives such as sustainable heritage management and eco-conscious restoration projects, Malta aims to strike a balance between tourism development and environmental conservation.

To raise awareness and encourage responsible behavior among tourists, Malta has launched educational campaigns and initiatives focused on promoting sustainable tourism practices. These efforts emphasize the significance of minimizing waste, respecting local cultures, and preserving the natural environment. Moreover, initiatives promoting responsible diving, marine conservation, and coastal clean-up programs have been instrumental in safeguarding Malta's marine ecosystem.

By fostering a culture of responsible tourism, Malta has positioned itself as a leading advocate for sustainable travel practices. Through its ongoing commitment to environmental initiatives, the country continues to set an example for other tourist destinations, demonstrating that the preservation of natural resources and cultural heritage is essential to the tourism sector's long-term viability.

# Responsible Tourism Tips

Responsible tourism involves making mindful choices that minimize the negative impacts of travel on the environment, local communities, and cultural heritage. Here are some detailed tips for practicing responsible tourism:

Respect Local Cultures and Customs: Familiarize yourself with the local customs, traditions, and social norms of the destination you plan to visit. Show respect for the local culture by dressing appropriately, learning a few phrases in the local language, and understanding the cultural sensitivities.

Support Local Businesses and Communities: Opt for locally-owned accommodations, restaurants, and tour operators to contribute to the economic growth of the community. Engage with local artisans and purchase authentic handicrafts or products, thereby directly supporting the local economy.

Minimize Environmental Impact: Reduce your carbon footprint by choosing eco-friendly transportation options such as public transit, biking, or walking. Conserve energy and water by being mindful of your consumption habits, such as turning off lights and limiting water usage in accommodations.

Reduce Plastic Usage: Carry a reusable water bottle, shopping bag, and utensils to minimize the use of single-use plastics. Dispose of waste responsibly in designated recycling bins or waste disposal facilities, and participate in local clean-up initiatives if available.

Protect Natural Resources: Respect wildlife and their habitats by avoiding activities that exploit or harm animals. Choose responsible wildlife tours and experiences that prioritize the well-being and conservation of the local fauna and flora.

Be Mindful of Cultural Heritage Sites: Follow designated trails, respect historical sites, and refrain from damaging or removing artifacts. Learn about the historical significance of the sites you visit and contribute to their preservation by adhering to the rules and regulations set by local authorities.

Contribute to Conservation Efforts: Consider volunteering for local conservation projects or donating to organizations dedicated to environmental and community initiatives. Participate in eco-tourism activities that support conservation efforts, such as tree planting, beach clean-ups, or wildlife protection programs.

Educate Yourself and Others: Stay informed about the destination's environmental challenges and cultural issues, and educate yourself on sustainable tourism practices. Share your knowledge and experiences with fellow travelers to promote awareness and encourage responsible travel behavior.

By incorporating these comprehensive responsible tourism tips into your travel plans, you can contribute to the preservation of local cultures, protect natural environments, and support the sustainable development of the destinations you visit.

# Supporting Local Communities

Supporting local communities is crucial for fostering sustainable development and promoting socio-economic growth in various regions around the world. When travelers actively engage with and support local communities during their visits, they contribute to the empowerment and well-being of the people living in these areas. Here are some ways to support local communities during your travels:

Choose Locally-Owned Businesses: Opt for accommodations, restaurants, and shops that are locally owned and operated. By patronizing these establishments, you directly contribute to the economic stability and growth of the community, allowing locals to benefit from tourism-related income and employment opportunities.

Participate in Cultural Experiences: Embrace cultural immersion by engaging in local activities, festivals, and events. Participate in cultural workshops, traditional performances, and cooking classes to gain a deeper understanding of the community's heritage and traditions. This not only enriches your travel experience but also provides direct financial support to local artisans and performers.

Purchase Authentic Local Products: Invest in locally-made handicrafts, artworks, and products that reflect the region's unique cultural identity. By buying directly from local artisans and producers, you contribute to the preservation of traditional crafts and skills, helping to sustain their livelihoods and preserve their cultural heritage.

Support Community-Based Tourism Initiatives: Seek out community-based tourism projects and initiatives that directly involve and benefit local residents. Participate in community tours led by knowledgeable locals, and contribute to community development projects, such as schools, health clinics, or infrastructure improvements, through donations or volunteer work.

Respect Local Customs and Traditions: Show respect for the customs and traditions of the local community by familiarizing yourself with their practices and norms. Be mindful of cultural sensitivities, dress codes, and social etiquette to demonstrate your appreciation for their way of life and foster positive cultural exchange.

Engage with the Local Population: Interact with locals in a respectful and friendly manner, showing genuine interest in their lives, stories, and perspectives. Take the time to learn about their daily routines, challenges, and aspirations, fostering meaningful connections that go beyond the tourist-local dynamic.

Contribute to Community Development: Support local community development initiatives, such as education, healthcare, and infrastructure projects, by donating to reputable local organizations or participating in volunteer programs that directly benefit the community. By contributing to sustainable development efforts, you can help improve the quality of life for the local population and contribute to long-term positive change.

By actively supporting local communities through these detailed practices, travelers can make a significant and positive impact on the social, cultural, and economic well-being of the places they visit, fostering a more sustainable and inclusive tourism industry.

# CONCLUSION

Malta's allure as a multifaceted destination is undeniable, as it seamlessly combines a rich historical tapestry with stunning natural beauty and a vibrant contemporary atmosphere. Whether it's exploring the ancient temples, indulging in the Mediterranean cuisine, or basking in the island's pristine beaches, Malta offers an unforgettable experience for travelers of all inclinations. With its warm hospitality, fascinating cultural heritage, and breathtaking landscapes, a journey to Malta is sure to leave an indelible mark on any adventurous soul seeking a truly immersive travel experience.

Malta, a gem nestled in the heart of the Mediterranean, is a vibrant and captivating destination that seamlessly blends a rich historical tapestry with stunning natural beauty and a modern, bustling atmosphere. This archipelago nation, consisting of three islands - Malta, Gozo, and Comino, is renowned for its rich cultural heritage, scenic coastlines, and warm hospitality. A journey to Malta offers travelers an immersive experience, where they can delve into ancient history, indulge in delectable Mediterranean cuisine, and soak in the sun on its pristine beaches. As we conclude this comprehensive travel guide to Malta, let us delve deeper into the enchanting allure and myriad offerings of this captivating destination.

Malta's history is a testament to its rich and diverse cultural influences, shaped by the Phoenicians, Romans, Moors, Knights of St. John, and the British Empire, among others. This historical backdrop has left an indelible mark on the Maltese archipelago, visible in its ancient temples, grand fortifications, and charming old towns. The UNESCO World Heritage sites of Ħal Saflieni Hypogeum, a subterranean necropolis dating back to 4000 BC, and the megalithic temples of Ġgantija in Gozo, dating back to 3600-3200 BC, stand as testaments to Malta's rich prehistoric legacy. Exploring these historical wonders provides a profound insight into the island's ancient past and its significance in the wider context of world history.

Beyond its historical marvels, Malta entices travelers with its stunning natural landscapes, ranging from dramatic cliffs and hidden coves to crystal-clear waters and golden beaches. The Blue Lagoon in Comino, with its azure waters and pristine white sands, is a true natural wonder that beckons visitors seeking a paradisiacal escape. The picturesque coastline and rugged terrain of Gozo offer panoramic vistas and opportunities for exhilarating outdoor adventures, such as hiking, diving, and snorkeling. Additionally, the charming countryside of Malta, adorned with terraced fields, quaint villages, and olive groves, provides a serene retreat for those wishing to immerse themselves in the island's rustic beauty.

A crucial aspect of any travel experience is savoring the local flavors, and Malta offers a delightful culinary journey that reflects its diverse cultural influences. From traditional dishes like rabbit stew (Fenkata) and pastizzi, flaky pastries filled with ricotta or mushy peas, to fresh seafood delicacies, the Maltese cuisine is a tantalizing fusion of Mediterranean, North African, and Sicilian flavors. The bustling food markets and family-run eateries scattered across the islands present an opportunity for travelers to indulge in authentic Maltese gastronomy and immerse themselves in the local culinary culture.

The Maltese hospitality, characterized by warmth, friendliness, and a strong sense of community, plays a pivotal role in enhancing the overall travel experience. The locals' genuine hospitality and eagerness to share their culture and traditions with visitors create a welcoming atmosphere that fosters meaningful connections and lasting memories. Whether engaging in lively conversations with the affable locals, participating in traditional festivities, or exploring the vibrant arts and music scene, travelers are sure to feel embraced by the Maltese spirit and find a sense of belonging in this captivating destination.

A journey to Malta is a holistic experience that transcends mere sightseeing, offering travelers an immersive encounter with history, nature, cuisine, and the vibrant local culture. The juxtaposition of ancient marvels with contemporary attractions, the tranquility of its natural landscapes with the bustling energy of its towns, and the warmth of its people with the richness of its traditions create an enriching tapestry that leaves a lasting impression on all who venture to this captivating archipelago. Malta, with its timeless allure and multifaceted offerings, is undoubtedly a destination that caters to the wanderlust of all kinds of travelers, making it an unforgettable gem in the Mediterranean.

Printed in Great Britain
by Amazon